THE WELSH REVIVAL

I
A NARRATIVE FACTS

BY W.T STEAD

II

THE REVIVAL: ITS POWER AND SOURCE

BY G.CAMPBELL MORGAN
"Behold I bring you good tidings of great joy"

Contents

I
A Narrative of Facts

II
The Revival :

I
A Narrative of Facts

The Welsh Revival

CHAPTER I

FROM THE AUTHOR TO THE READER

THIS is the reason why this little book is written :

I am a child of the revival of 1859–60. I have witnessed the revival in South Wales, and it is borne in upon me that I must testify as to what I have seen and know.

I have been urged and entreated to speak in public on the subject. I have refused, although sorely tempted to comply. But though I am not physically strong enough to face the immense strain which public speaking always makes upon my nervous system, I cannot keep silent. Woe is me if I bear not my testimony, and bear it now ! For never is it so true as in times of revival that "Now is the accepted time ; now is the day of salvation."

That is not a mere hackneyed text ; it is a somewhat awe-inspiring fact. A fact, not a theory. The importance of the psychological moment so much insisted upon by Bismarck is as true in religion as in politics. It is the familiar truth, which all admit in other departments of life.

> " There is a tide in the affairs of men
> Which, taken at the flood, leads on to fortune.
> Omitted, all the voyage of their life
> Is bound in shallows, and in miseries."

Let me preface my narrative, as is the custom in all meetings when the awakened soul cries for facts from the experience of living men rather than for things at second-hand, by stating briefly how I came to be able to speak with knowledge of the mysterious force operating upon the heart of men which is in action at times of revival.

I first woke up to a sense of my own sinfulness when I was a child of eleven. I was a child of the manse. My father was an Independent minister, and both my parents were earnest, devoted evangelical Christians. Independents sixty years ago were more Calvinistic than are their present-day representatives, and a sense of the exceeding sinfulness of sin and of the grim reality of the wrath of God permeated the atmosphere of our home. The higher the ideal of life and conduct to which we were taught to aspire, the more bitterly and constantly we were compelled to realize by every childish fault of selfishness or of temper how true it was that we had all sinned and come short of the glory of God. We were condemned by our own consciences. Even when we would do good, evil was present with us. How could we, with all our imperfections, our sins and our shortcomings, think without a shudder of the day when all secrets were revealed, and the soul, stripped bare of all wrappings and pretence, had to render account to its Maker for all the deeds that had been done in the body? It is the fashion of our day to regard such striving after the Ideal as morbid ; but although the phraseology may need revision, the essential truth remains the same.

It is not surprising, then, that one night, at eleven years of age, when I went to bed, I was seized with an appalling sense of my own unworthiness, my own exceeding sinfulness. God was so good, and I was so bad—I deserved to be damned. I accepted as a postulate the infinite goodness

of God, and I knew only too well how often I had done
the things I ought not to have done, and left undone
the things I ought to have done, and that there was no
strength in me. I sobbed and cried in the darkness with a
vague sense of my own sin and of the terrible doom which
awaited me. I had a passionate longing to escape from
condemnation and be forgiven. At last my mother over-
heard me, took me into her arms, and told me comforting
things about the love of God, and how it was made manifest by Jesus Christ, who had suffered in our stead, to save
us from condemnation and make us heirs of heaven. I
have no remembrance of anything beyond the soothing ca-
ress of my mother's words. When she left me the terror
had gone; and although I had not in any way experienced
the change which is called conversion, I felt sufficiently
tranquil to go to sleep. When I woke the memory of the
previous night's alarm was but as the remembrance of a
thunder-storm when it has passed.

This was in the year 1860, when the revival which had
begun in the United States of America in 1857 or 1858
crossed the Atlantic, traversed the north of Ireland in
1858, covered Wales in 1859, and then moved into
England, where its influence was felt all through 1860
and 1861.

In July, 1861, I was sent to a boarding-school for Congregational ministers' sons, to which some sons of laymen
were also admitted, at Silcoates Hall, near Wakefield.
There were about fifty of us boys, from ten years old to six-
teen or seventeen. The tradition of the school in the fifties
and in 1860 had not been distinctly religious. All of us
came from Christian homes, but as a school it was very
much like other schools. About a month after I entered
Silcoates some of the lads started a prayer-meeting of their
own in a summer-house in the garden. They asked me to

join, and I went more out of curiosity, and to oblige my
chum, than from any other motive. There were about half a
dozen of us, perhaps more, none of us over fourteen. We
read a chapter in the Bible, and we prayed. No master
was present, nor was there any attempt made on the part of
the masters to encourage the prayer-meeting. One master,
indeed, was frankly contemptuous. The majority of the
boys had nothing to do with " the prayer-meeting fellows."
One or two of us were under deep conviction of sin, and we
talked among ourselves, and read the Bible, and prayed.
Suddenly, one day, after the prayer-meeting had been going
on for a week or two, there seemed to be a sudden change
in the atmosphere. How it came about no one ever knew.
All that we did know was that there seemed to have de-
scended from the sky, with the suddenness of a drenching
thunder-shower, a spirit of intense, earnest seeking after God
for the forgiveness of sins and consecration to his service.
The summer-house was crowded with boys. A deputation
waited upon the principal, and told him what was happen-
ing. He was very sympathetic and helpful. Preparation
class was dispensed with that night ; all the evening
the prayer-meeting was kept going. There was no singing, only Bible reading, a few brief words of exhortation,
a confession of sin, and asking for prayers, and ever and
anon a joyful acknowledgment of an assurance of forgiveness. Those of us who could not find peace were taken out
into the playground by one or two of their happier comrades,
who labored with them to accept Christ. How well to this
very day do I remember the solemn hush of that memorable
day and night, in the course of which forty out of the fifty
lads publicly professed conversion. Only half a dozen out
of the whole school, and these exclusively of the oldest boys,
held aloof from the movement, and were prayed for jointly
and severally by name by their converted comrades.

I remember the way in which it came to me that my
sins were forgiven, and that from being a rebel against
God I was admitted into the family of the redeemed.
I had no ecstasy. Alas! my temperament is not subject
to ecstasies. My friend, a lad of my own age, was
walking by my side plying me diligently with texts,
and appealing to me to believe only in Christ. As we
walked and talked together it slowly seemed to dawn
upon my mind that I had been saved all the time, and
had never known it till just then—saved not by any
merit of my own, but because in some mysterious way,
positively asserted in the New Testament, and verified by
the experience of all the best human beings whom I knew or
had heard of, the death of Christ had reconciled the world
to God. He had borne my sins, therefore they were no
longer on record against me. There was no condemnation
for those who were in Christ Jesus. And who were "in
Christ Jesus"? The whole human race, excepting those
who thrust themselves out of his fold and would none of
him. In short, it seemed to me that I had always inverted
the position. Instead of thinking I had to do some strange
spiritual act described as "coming to Jesus," when my sins
would be forgiven and I should be adopted as a son of God,
I came to see that Christ had already reconciled me to God,
had forgiven my sins, thousands of years before they had
been committed, and that I had just to accept the position
in which he had graciously placed me. Of my own self
I could have done nothing. I was a sinner, not only in the
sight of God, but in my own inner consciousness. I had
been made in the image of God, and had unmade myself
into the image of a very ordinary, bad-tempered, selfish
lad, not perhaps more bad-tempered or more selfish than
other twelve-year-old lads, but a very ordinary sinner, not
by any means the saint and the hero which I ought to have

been. I was a poor wretch, but God in his unspeakable love and mercy had blotted out my sins, and taken me into junior—very junior—partnership with himself. The terms were, on my side, that I had to do what he told me, and, on his side, that he would tell me quite clearly what he wanted me to do. And although I had no ecstasy, and was gladdened by no heavenly vision, a sense of great peace and deliverance settled upon me.

I was seized with the longing to tell others of the discovery I had made—that we were saved all the time if we only knew it, and that God was a great deal more anxious to take us into partnership than we were to accept so gracious an offer. Writing was a sore cross to me, *ætat* 12, but I wrote to my parents and told them the good news. I wrote to my elder sister, urging her to be converted. We had prayer circles for the conversion of our unconverted comrades. In the fervor of my boyish zeal I decided to be a missionary, and applied myself all the more diligently to my lessons. About twenty of us joined the church as communicants. Every night during the two years I was at Silcoates the prayer-meeting was kept up by the lads. Half an hour after tea, before preparation, was given to the prayer-meeting. But—and this brings me to the point of all this confession of personal experience—although the tone of the school was kept up at a high level, and although the prayer-meeting was kept going, and the solid fruits of the revival lasted all the time I was there, we never had another conversion after that strange outpouring of the Spirit which overwhelmed us all, unexpectant, at the beginning of the term. Those who were brought in during the revival week stood for the most part firm; those who stood out against the revival never came in afterward. Neither, so far as I remember, with perhaps one or two exceptions, did the new lads who entered school later on seek or find conversion.

I am not setting forth the conception of the relation between man and his Maker embodied in the foregoing narrative as if it were the truth of God to any other soul excepting my own. And for those who deny both God and the soul, I am willing, for the sake of argument, to admit that the whole episode in my life was nothing more or less than the delusion of something that imagined itself to be a soul as to the reality of its relations with a nullity which it imagined was its Creator. The truth or the falsehood of my notions is, in this immediate connection, quite immaterial. For what I am wanting to insist upon is, first, that these seasons of spiritual exaltation which we call revivals are realities to those who come under their influence, permanently affecting their whole future lives; and, secondly, that they come like the wind and vanish as mysteriously, and that those who resist them may never again feel so potent a call to a higher life.

It is this sense of the fact that the revival, when it comes, does not stop but passes on, which fills me with such a sense of the infinite importance of this present time, that I feel I must do what I can to bring to the knowledge of as many persons as I can reach, the glad tidings of great joy that a revival of religion is once more in our midst.

The old story of the man who was gathering eggs from the face of a precipitous cliff always recurs to me at such seasons of opportunity. The man, clinging to a rope, had lowered himself from the overhanging edge of a beetling cliff, till he was opposite the ledge where the sea-birds laid their eggs. Owing to the extent to which the brow of the cliff overhung the sea, whose waves were dashing 200 feet below, the egg-gatherer found himself some ten feet distant from the ledge of the nests. By swaying to and fro, he was able to make himself swing as a pendulum outward and inward, until at last the extreme inward swing of the rope brought him to the ledge, onto which he sprang. As he did so he lost hold of the rope. There he stood for one awful moment midway between sea and sky. The rope, swinging outward after he had quitted his hold, was returning like a pendulum. It came, but not so far as to enable him to clutch it from where he stood. Outward it swung again, and he realized with agony that as each time it swayed to and fro it would be further and further off, until at last it would hang stationary far out of his reach. When the rope began slowly to swing inwards, he saw that the next time it would be out of his reach. Breathless, he waited until the rope was just about to pause before swinging back, then, knowing that it was now or never, he leaped into space, caught the rope, and was saved. Another second and he would have lost his chance. It is just so, it seems to me, with revivals. They come and they go, and if they are not utilized the opportunity goes by—in some cases forever.

For the churches the revival is like spring. The good seed sown then springs up and bears fruit, whereas ten times the quantity of seed sown in winter's frost or summer's heat would simply perish. But in these prefatory observations I am not thinking of the churches so much as of the individual reader who does not believe, who is not converted, and who is only idly curious as to whether there is anything in "this revival business," or whether there is not. It is for them that I have told, for the first time in my life, the story of how a revival affected me, and what I know of it at first hand. And there is one other point upon which I think I may fairly claim to speak at first hand, and that is as to the effect of that experience at Silcoates in 1861 upon my own life. Whatever may be the objective reality of the altered relations which I then recognized as existing between my soul and its Maker, there is absolutely no question as to the abiding nature of the change it effected in my life. It is forty-three years since that revival at school. The whole of my life during all these forty-three years has been influenced by the change which men call conversion which occurred with me when I was twelve. My views as to many things have naturally broadened much in these forty-three years, but that was the conscious starting-point of everything that there has been in my life of good or of service for my fellow creatures. It was my first conversion. Other spiritual experiences, involving a wider conception of the reality of God in man, a deeper sense of the need for self-surrender, I have had, and hope yet to have. But the fundamental change, the conscious recognition of the fact that I had been most graciously allotted a junior partnership with God Almighty in the great task of making this world a little bit more like heaven than it is to-day, came to me then. My life has been flawed with many failures, darkened with many sins, but the thing in it which was good, which has enabled me to resist temptations to which I would otherwise have succumbed, to bear burdens which would otherwise have crushed me with their weight, and which has kept the soul within me ever joyfully conscious that, despite all appearances to the contrary, this is God's world, and that he and I are fellow workers in the work of its renovation—that potent thing, whatever you may call it, and however you may explain it, came into my life then, and abides with me to this hour—my one incentive and inspiration in this life; my sole hope for that which is to come.

Therefore I hope my reader will understand how it is that I, being a child of the revival of 1858 to 1861, should hail with exceeding great joy the reappearance of the revival in 1904. For as the mysterious outpouring of the blessing forty-three years ago has been of permanent help and strength and comfort to my own life ever since that time, so will this revival in Wales change, transform, inspire and glorify the lives of multitudes who at present know nothing and care nothing for the things that make for their own peace and the welfare of their fellow men.

And the thought that haunts me and will not let me rest until I send out this little book is that if I do not write it, and write it now, you, my reader, may not hear the bugle call which is sounding in Wales ; the revival may pass by, and, too late, you may awake to discover that you have missed the gift of God which it bore for your soul.

CHAPTER II

THE NATIONAL SIGNIFICANCE OF REVIVALS

> Slowly the Bible of the race is writ,
> And not on paper leaves nor leaves of stone.
> Each age, each kindred adds a verse to it,
> Texts of despair or hope, of joy or moan ;
> While swings the sea, while mists the mountains shroud,
> While thunders' surges burst on cliffs of cloud,
> Still at the prophet's feet the nations sit.—*Lowell.*

ONE of these newly written verses is spelling itself out before our eyes in Wales. In order to understand its significance we need to look backward across some centuries to realize what vast issues may be in this upheaval among the Welsh country folk.

The word revival is not to be found in the index to the latest edition of the " Encyclopædia Britannica." Neither does it figure in the comprehensive index to Baring-Gould's " Lives of the Saints." Yet the Saints were great revivalists, and the history of the progress of the world is largely made up of the record of successive revivals. The revival of religion has been the invariable precursor of social and political reform. This was very admirably put by the Rev. F. B. Meyer in his Presidential Address to the Ninth National Council of the Evangelical Free Churches at Newcastle-on-Tyne in 1904.

Every great revival of religion has issued in social and political reconstruction. In no history has the effect of the one upon the other been more carefully traced than in Green's " History of the English People." Take, for in-

stance, his account of the revival of the twelfth century.
"At the close of Henry's reign," he says, "and throughout
that of Stephen, England was stirred by the first of those
great religious movements, which it was afterward to experience in the preaching of the Friars, the Lollardism of
Wycliffe, the Reformation, the Puritan enthusiasm, and the
mission work of the Wesleys. Everywhere, in town and
country, men banded themselves together for prayer;
hermits flocked to the woods; noble and churl welcomed
the austere Cistercians as they spread over the moors and
forests of the North. A new spirit of devotion woke the
slumbers of the religious houses, and penetrated alike to the
homes of the noble and the trader. The power of this revival eventually became strong enough to wrest England
from the chaos of feudal misrule after a long period of
feudal anarchy, and laid the foundations of the Great
Charta." We may go further, and assert that the movements which led to the abolition of the Slave Trade and the
Corn Laws originated in the evangelistic efforts of Wesley
and Whitefield. Even Mr. Benjamin Kidd, in his "Social
Evolution," lays great stress on the religious foundations
upon which civilization rests. He tells us that the intellect
has always mistaken the nature of religious forces, and regarded them as beneath its notice, though they had within
them power to control the course of human development for
hundreds and even thousands of years. Discussing the op-
position of the educated classes in England to progress, he
says: "The motive force behind the long list of progressive
measures has not, to any appreciable extent, come from the
educated classes—it has come almost exclusively from the
middle and lower classes, who have in turn acted, not under
the stimulus of intellectual motives, but under the influence
of their religious feelings." It is, therefore, on the authority
of history and economics that we base our contention that
society can only be saved through a great revival of religion.

There are certain phenomena which precede and which
follow revivals of religion. The symptoms premonitory of
a revival are the phenomena of death, corruption and decay.

It is ever the darkest hour before the dawn. The nation always seems to be given over to the Evil One before the coming of the Son of Man. The decay of religious faith, the deadness of the churches, the atheism of the well-to-do, the brutality of the masses, all these, when at their worst, herald the approach of the revival. Things seem to get too bad to last. The reign of evil becomes intolerable. Then the soul of the nation awakes.

That the familiar phenomena of the reign of sin are with us and abound, no serious observer will dispute. As a nation we have once more stooped to those depths of bloody mire in which from time to time Britain has wallowed. Drunkenness, gambling and gluttony, with others of the seven deadly sins, abound. Worldliness is universal. High ideals are eclipsed. Plain living and high thinking are at a discount. To see as in a mirror the vacuous mind of a generation which eschews serious thought you have only to read the popular newspapers and periodicals of the day.

Life has become for the comfortable classes little better than a musical comedy. You look in vain for the strenuous, high-spirited youth who scorn delights and live laborious days in order to achieve something of good for their fellow men. To have a good time is the end-all and be-all of millions. Indolence, indifference and selfishness so dominate that even the healthy game of football has become little better than a modern substitute for the gladiatorial sports of ancient Rome—the winter gambling-hell that replaces the summer race-course. Our young men do not play themselves; they look on while professionals play.

In politics degradation shows itself chiefly in the indifference to bloodshed and the waste of the resources of our own people in making believe to be ready to slaughter our neighbors. As a condemnation alike of the morality and intellect of the nation, the army and navy expenditure of Britain

for the last twelve years stands without a parallel.   Here
we have the very note of the decadence of our time.   That
way madness lies, and the supreme and crowning demon-
stration of the criminal lunacy which has overtaken us is
afforded by the proposal to tax the bread and sugar of the
poor in order to meet the demands of insatiate Mars.

If, therefore, a revival never comes until the nation has
sunk into the slough of luxury and vice, and wallows in
brutality and crime, then this precursory symptom is as-
suredly not wanting in the present situation.   It is interest-
ing to turn over the pages of Green's " History of the
English People," and to note how invariably the revival is
preceded by a period of corruption and followed by a great
advance in the direction of national progress.

Take, for instance, what he tells us about the state of
England on the eve of the second revival.   The effect of the
first revival had passed away by the middle of the thirteenth
century.   The second was brought about by the Franciscans
and the Dominicans.

Speaking of the coming of the Friars, Mr. Green
says :

The religious hold of the priesthood on the people was
loosening day by day.   .   .   .   The disuse of preaching,
the decline of the monastic orders into rich landowners, the
non-residence and ignorance of the parish priests, robbed
the clergy of their spiritual influence.   The abuses of the
times foiled even the energy of such men as Bishop Grosseteste, of Lincoln.   To bring the world back again within
the pale of the Church was the aim of two religious orders
which sprang suddenly into life in the opening of the
thirteenth century.

He then describes how the revival due to the Black
Friars of St. Dominic and the Gray Friars of St. Francis
swept in a great tide of popular enthusiasm over the land.

They carried the gospel to the poor by the entire reversal of the older monasticism by seeking personal salvation in effort for the salvation of their fellow men. Their fervid appeal, coarse wit and familiar story brought religion into the fair and the market-place. They captured the University of Oxford, and made it stand in the front line in its resistance to Papal exactions and its claim of English liberty.

The classes in the towns on whom the influence of the Friars told most directly were the steady supporters of freedom throughout the Barons' War. Adam Marsh was the closest friend and confidant both of Grosseteste and Earl Simon of Montfort.

Thus, if the first revival preceded the signing of the Magna Charta, the second paved the way for the assembly of the first English Parliament.

The third revival mentioned by Green was that of Wycliffe. The second revival had spent its force in a hundred years. The Church of the Middle Ages had, at the middle of the fourteenth century, sunk to its lowest point of spiritual decay. The clergy were worldly and corrupt, and paralyzed by their own dissensions. The early enthusiasm of the Friars had died away, leaving a crowd of impudent mendicants behind. Then Wycliffe arose. He recalled the ideal of " the Kingdom of God " before the eyes of mankind, and established his order of " Simple Priests " or Poor Preachers, who, with coarse speech and russet dress, preached the gospel throughout the land with such success that the enemy declared in alarm that " every second man one meets is a Lollard." Wycliffe died, but the seed he had sowed sprang up and bore terrible fruit in the Peasant Revolt, which, although ultimately trampled out in bloodshed, was the first great warning given to the landlords of England that the serf not only had the rights of man, but was capable on occasion of asserting them, even by such extreme measures as the decapitation of an archbishop.

The fourth revival was that which preceded the Reformation. Tyndale, with his translation of the Bible, blew upon the smouldering embers of Lollardry and they burst into flame. The new Scriptures were disputed, rimed, sung, and jangled in every tavern and ale-house. From that revival of popular religion among the masses came by tortuous roads the triumph of Protestantism.

After the Reformation and the Renaissance had achieved their culminating glory in the reign of Queen Elizabeth, a period of decadence and of corruption set in under the Stuarts. Under James I, Whitehall became an Augean stable of all uncleanness, and a vicious Court assailed the liberties of England. Against this corruption in high places a fierce religious rebellion broke out amongst the serious English folk. The Puritan Revival of the first half of the seventeenth century had two notable offshoots. The first was the founding of New England by the men of the *Mayflower;* the other was the founding of the English Commonwealth by the Ironsides of Cromwell. The great struggle of the seventeenth century was primarily religious, only secondarily political. As Green remarks, "There was one thing dearer in England than free speech in Parliament, than security for property, or even personal liberty, and that one thing was, in the phrase of the day, the Gospel." It was the religious revival that summoned Milton from literature to politics. So long as the question between king and parliament was purely political, he shut himself up with his books and "calmly awaited the issue of the contest, which I trusted to the wise conduct of Providence and to the courage of the people." But when men began to demand the reforming of the Church in accordance with the Word of God, Milton tells us in his " Second Defence of the People of England " :

> This awakened all my attention and my zeal. I saw that a way was opening for the establishment of real liberty, that the foundation was laying for the deliverance of man from the yoke of slavery and superstition, that the principles of religion, which were the first objects of our care, would exert a salutary influence on the manners and constitution of the republic: and as I had from my youth studied the distinction between religious and civil rights, I perceived that if I ever wished to be of use I ought at least not to be wanting to my country, to the Church, and to so many of my fellow-Christians in a crisis of so much danger. I therefore determined to relinquish the other pursuits in which I was engaged, and to transfer the whole force of my talents and industry to this one important subject.

Others besides Milton felt the imperious call of the religious movement of his time. Nor did its impulse fail until the death of Oliver Cromwell opened the door to the rabble rout of the Restoration.

Once more England plunged heavily toward the nethermost abyss, and once again a great revival of religion took place to save the soul of the nation from perdition. It was partly due to the relentless persecution of the Nonconformists, but it owed much also to the flaming zeal of the Quakers, who were the great revivalists of the second half of the seventeenth century. The government had at one time in horrible dungeons as many as four thousand of these excellent men. Professor William James truly says of the Quaker religion that it "is something which it is impossible to overpraise."

In a day of shams, it was a religion of veracity rooted

in spiritual inwardness and a return to something more like
the original Gospel truth than men had ever known in
England.   So far as our Christian sects to-day are evolving
into liberality, they are simply reverting in essence to the
position which Fox and the early Quakers so long ago
assumed.

6   The Quaker Revival had as its immediate political
result the founding of Pennsylvania, and among its more
remote and indirect effects the final expulsion of the Stuarts.

Quakerism, tolerated, lost much of the savory salt that it
possessed when it was kept up to the standard of the apostles
by the sufferings of the martyrs.   The reversion of the
English people, especially of the highest and the lowest, to
sheer paganism is one of the most constant phenomena of
our history.   After the Stuarts had vanished and the Prot-
estant succession secured, the land relapsed into brutality
and infidelity in the eighteenth century, as it had done in
every century since the Conquest.

7   Then came the seventh and best known revival of all
under Wesley and Whitefield.   Once again England had
gone rotten at the head.   " In the higher circles of society
every one laughs," said Montesquieu on his visit to England, " if one talks of religion.   Of the prominent statesmen
of the time, the greater part were unbelievers in any form of
Christianity, and distinguished for the grossness and im-
morality of their lives."   As at the top, so at the bottom.
The masses were brutalized beyond belief.   " In London,
at one time, gin-shops invited every passer-by to get drunk
for a penny, and dead drunk for twopence."   But in the
midst of this moral wilderness a religious revival sprang up
which carried to the hearts of the people a fresh spirit of
moral zeal, while it purified our literature and our manners.
" A new philanthropy reformed our prisons, infused clem-
ency and wisdom into our penal laws, abolished the slave

trade, and gave the first impulse to popular education."
The revival then was not without many features which
caused the sinner to blaspheme. "Women fell down in
convulsions; strong men were smitten suddenly to the earth;
the preacher was interrupted by bursts of hysteric laughter
or hysteric sobbing." Very foolish and absurd, no doubt,
sniggered the superior persons of that day. But if Mr.
Lecky and other observers may be believed, it was that foolishness of the Methodist revival that saved the children of
these superior persons from having their heads sheared off
by an outburst of revolutionary frenzy similar to that of the
Reign of Terror.

About the same time that Wesley was preaching in England a great revival broke out in Wales, of which one of
the outward and visible signs most plainly perceptible
among us to-day is the fact of the Welsh revolt against
the Education Act. That the Liberal party commands to-
day a solid majority among the Welsh members is the
direct result of the revival of 1759, which is associated
with the name of Howell Harris, a layman of the Church
of England, who, while taking part in the Litany in his
parish church, became suddenly filled with a fervent zeal,
and went forth to preach the gospel to his fellow men. At
first the movement was within the pale of the Church. Ten
beneficed clergymen were among the revivalists of that
day. What would have happened if the Anglican au-
thorities had possessed the wisdom of the serpent and had
followed the example of the Church of Rome in utilizing
the zeal of her enthusiasts to extend her own borders, who
can say? But the problem never arose. The Anglican
Church, true to its evil traditions, cast out the revivalists,
and Welsh Nonconformity was born. Modern Wales is
the direct product of the revival of the eighteenth century.

As a leading Baptist minister said, writing on this subject on November 19th :

The Nonconformist bodies of Wales owe their origin to religious revivals, two to that of the seventeenth century and two to that of the eighteenth century. Wales has to thank her past revivals for the greater part of the energy exhibited in her national, political and social life. In the revivals with which the people of Wales have been blessed of God, his Spirit engraved upon the conscience of the nation the terribly solemn truths of existence and the things which belong unto her peace. This gave to her men of conviction and of courage, and taught her to aspire to all that is good and noble, and whatever her achievements are religiously and socially, they are due mainly to the stimulus received during periods of outpouring of the Spirit of God.

In the nineteenth century the Tractarian Movement may be regarded by some as a revival. But it was neither preceded by great apathy nor followed by vigorous political progress. The most notable revival of the century was that which broke out in the United States in the latter end of the fifties, and which spread in a few years over Ulster and Wales, and from thence made its way into England and Scotland. The revival seems to travel in the opposite direction to the sun. The great revival of 1740, under Jonathan Edwards in New England, preceded by many years the Welsh revival under Howell Harris and the English revival under Wesley and Whitefield. In like manner the revival that touched Wales in 1859 and England in the early sixties had its birth in 1857 or 1858 across the Atlantic, where it was the direct precursor of the great civil war and the emancipation of the slaves. The revival of 1859 to 1861 coincided with the closing years of Whig domination, and was followed very speedily by a great movement of popular reform. There was no direct connection between the establishment of household suffrage and the penitent forms and prayer-meetings of 1859 and 1861. *Post hoc* is not *propter hoc*. But when reform follows revival, the plain man may be pardoned if he sees some connection between the two other than mere coincidence. The coincidence, if it be such, is surely very remarkable. The record of revivals in English history runs thus :—

	REVIVAL	RESULT
12th century	The Cistercian	Magna Charta
13th "	The Friars	Parliamentary Government
14th "	Wycliffe	The Peasant Revolt
16th "	Tyndale	The Reformation
17th "	Puritanism	The Fall of Despotism and the Founding of New England
17½th "	Quakerism	The Revolution of 1688 and the Founding of Pennsylvania
18th "	Methodist	The Era of Reform
19th "	American	The Era of Democracy
20th "	Welsh	Who can say ?

To the observer of the phenomena of national growth and the evolution of society these periodical revivals of religion are as marked a phenomenon in the history of England, possibly of other lands, as the processions of the seasons. To appreciate the prophetic significance of a religious revival does not necessarily involve any acceptance of the truth of the religion. All that we have to recognize is that the history of human progress in this country has always followed a certain course, which in its main features is as invariable as the great changes which make up our year. Always there is the winter of corruption, of luxury, of indolence, of vice, during which the nation seems to have forgotten God, and to have given itself up to drunkenness, gambling, avarice, and impurity. Men's hearts fail them for fear, and the love of many grows cold. It is the season when, through most of the day, the sun withholds his beams, and a bitter frost chills all the nobler aspirations of the soul. Through such a period of eclipse we have been passing during the last few years. But as the rainbow in the ancient story stands eternal in the heavens as a proof that summer and winter, seed-time and harvest, shall fail not, so after such periods of black and bitter wintry reaction always comes the gracious spring-tide with healing in its wings.

And, as we have seen, the outward and visible sign of the coming of spring in the history of the nation is a great revival of religious earnestness—a sudden and wide-spread outburst of evangelistic fervor. We may dislike many of its manifestations, as we dislike the winds of March or the showers of April, but they occur in almost identical fashion century after century. The form changes. The preaching of the Friars was not exactly the same as the preaching of the Methodists. Wycliffe's Poor Preachers and the Early Friends differed both in dialect and in doctrine. But at bottom all the English revivals have been identical. One and all represent the springtime of faith in the heart of man, a sudden rediscovery that life is given him not to please his senses, but to serve his Maker, and that time is but the vestibule of eternity. The sense of the reality of an ever-living God within, around, above, beneath, in whom we live and move and have our being, and the related sense of a never-dying soul, whose destiny throughout numberless eons of the future years will be influenced by the way in which each day of our mortal probation is spent —these two great truths are rediscovered afresh by the English people every century. The truths blossom in the national heart at these times of spiritual spring-tide as the hawthorn blossoms on the hedge in the merry month of May.

That the revival time passes is true. So passes spring-tide with its flowers. But as spring is followed by summer, so the revival of religion in this country has ever been followed by the summer of reform and the harvest of garnered fruit. It is this which ought to make every thoughtful person of all creeds, or of no creed, watch with the keenest interest the symptoms which indicate the coming of a national revival. Until this nation goes to the penitent form, it never really pulls itself together for any serious work.

CHAPTER III

WHAT I SAW IN WALES

THE first notice of the existence of the revival that appeared in the press was published on November 7, 1904. It was not until December 10 that I went down to Cardiff, and was joined there by the Rev. Thomas Law, the Organizing Secretary of the National Council, and Gipsy Smith, the evangelist, whom I had not seen since I bade him farewell at Cape Town. On Sunday we went over to the mining village of Mardy and attended three services at which Mr. Evan Roberts was present. I returned to Cardiff that evening and came on to London next morning.

As I wrote out before leaving Cardiff my report for *The Daily Chronicle*, where it appeared on December 13, was interviewed early on Tuesday morning for *The Methodist Times* of December 15, and wrote on Tuesday afternoon a report for *The Christian World* of December 15, I cannot do better than reprint here these first clear impressions of what I found going on in South Wales. I will quote the interview first because it brings out more abruptly and vividly what seems to me the supernatural side of the revival.

Interview in "The Methodist Times,"
December 15th.

"Well, Mr. Stead, you 've been to the revival. What do you think of it?"

"Sir," said Mr. Stead, "the question is not what I think of it, but what it thinks of me, of you, and all the rest of us. For it is a very real thing, this revival: a live thing which seems to have a power and a grip which may get hold of a good many of us who at present are mere spectators."

" Do you think it is on the march, then ? "

" A revival is something like a revolution. It is apt to be wonderfully catching. But you can never say. Look at the way the revolutionary tempest swept over Europe in 1848. But since then revolutions have not spread much beyond the border of the state in which they break out. We may have become immune to revivals, gospel-hardened or totally indifferent. I do n't think so. But I would not like to prophesy."

" But in South Wales the revival is moving ? "

" It reminded me," said Mr. Stead, " of the effect which travelers say is produced on the desert by the winds which propel the sand-storms, beneath which whole caravans have been engulfed. The wind springs up, no one knows from whence. Its eddying gusts lick up the sands, and soon the whole desert is filled with moving columns of sand, swaying and dancing and whirling as if they were instinct with life. Woe be to the unprotected traveler whose path the sand-storm traverses."

" Then do you feel that we are in the track of the storm ? "

" Can our people sing ? That is the question to be answered before you can decide that. Hitherto the revival has not strayed beyond the track of the singing people. It has followed the line of song, not of preaching. It has sung its way from one end of South Wales to the other. But, then, the Welsh are a nation of singing birds."

" You speak as if you dreaded the revival coming your way ? "

" No, that is not so. Dread is not the right word. Awe expresses my sentiment better. For you are in the presence of the unknown. I tell you it is a live thing this revival, and if it gets hold of the people in London, for instance, it will make a pretty considerable shaking up."

" But surely it will be all to the good ? "

" Yes, for the good or for those who are all good. But what about those who are not good, or who, like the most of us, are a pretty mixed lot? Henry Ward Beecher used to say that if God were to answer the Lord's Prayer and cause his will to be done in earth as it is in heaven, there were streets in New York which would be wrecked as if they had been struck by a tornado. Of course, it may be all to the good that we should be all shaken up, and tornadoes clear the air ; earthquakes are wholesome, but they are not particularly welcome to those who are at ease in Zion."

"Sand-storms in the desert, tornadoes, earthquakes ! Really, Mr. Stead, your metaphors would imply that your experiences in South Wales have been pretty bad ? "

" No," said Mr. Stead, " not bad at all. Do you remember what the little Quaker child said, when the Scottish express rushed at full speed through the station on the platform on which he was standing ? ' Were you not frightened, my boy ? ' said his father. ' Oh, no,' said the little chap, ' a feeling of sweet peace stole into my mind.' I felt like that rather. But the thing is awesome. You do n't believe in ghosts ? "

" Not much. I 'll believe them when I see one."

"Well, you have read ghost stories, and can imagine what you would feel if you were alone at midnight in the haunted chamber of some old castle, and you heard slow and stealthy steps stealing along the corridor where the visitant from the other world was said to walk. If you go to South Wales and watch the revival you will feel pretty much like that. There is something there from the Other World. You cannot say whence it came or whither it is going, but

it moves and lives and reaches for you all the time. You
see men and women go down in sobbing agony before your
eyes as the invisible Hand clutches at their hearts. And
you shudder. It's pretty grim, I tell you. If you are
afraid of strong emotions you'd better give the revival a
wide berth."

"But is it all emotion? Is there no teaching?"

"Precious little. Do you think that teaching is what
people want in a revival? These people, all the people in a
land like ours, are taught to death, preached to insensibility.
They all know the essential truths. They know that they
are not living as they ought to live, and no amount of teaching will add anything to that conviction. To hear some
people talk you would imagine that the best way to get a
sluggard out of bed is to send a tract on astronomy showing
him that according to the fixed and eternal law the sun will
rise at a certain hour in the morning. The sluggard does
not deny it. He is entirely convinced of it. But what he
knows is that it is precious cold at sunrise on a winter's
morning, and it is very snug and warm between the blankets.
What the sluggard needs is to be well shaken, and in case of
need to be pulled out of bed. ' Roused,' the revival calls
it. And the revival is a rouser rather than a teacher. And
that is why I think those churches which want to go on
dozing in the ancient ways had better hold a special series
of prayer-meetings that the revival may be prevented coming
their way."

"Then I take it that your net impressions were favorable?"

"How could they be otherwise? Did I not feel the pull
of that unseen Hand? And have I not heard the glad outburst of melody that hailed the confession of some who in
very truth had found salvation? There is a wonderful
spontaneity about it all, and so far its fruits have been good,
and only good."

" Will it last ? "

" Nothing lasts forever in this mutable world, and the revival will no more last than the blossom lasted in the field in springtime. But if the blossom had not come and gone, there would be no bread in the world to-day. And as it is with the bread which Mr. Chamberlain would tax, so it is with that other bread which is the harvest that will be gathered in long after this revival has taken its place in history. But if the analogy of all previous revivals holds good, this religious awakening will be influencing for good the lives of numberless men and women who will be living and toiling and carrying on the work of this God's world of ours long after you and I have been gathered to our fathers. "

The report which I wrote for *The Christian World* was written for people inside the churches, who might naturally be supposed to be interested in the reality of the spiritual side of the revival.

From " The Christian World,"
December 15th.

Will the revival in South Wales be like a bonfire on ice or will it set the heather afire, kindling a blaze which no man can extinguish ? The answer is that no one can prophesy confidently as to what the future may bring to us, excepting that it will always both disappoint and exceed our expectations. The revival in Wales will, in some places, be like a bonfire on ice, which speedily expires for lack of fuel, and yet in other places it may set the heather on fire and produce quite incalculable results.

I cannot profess to have made any exhaustive study of the revival. Until last Saturday I had only followed it in the newspapers. But from Saturday night till Monday

morning I employed every available moment in observing
it and in interviewing those who had been in it from the
first. I was accompanied throughout the whole of my brief
tour by two men who have had as much experience of mission work of a revivalist nature as any one outside the Salvation Army. One of them, Gipsy Smith, had come over
the same day as I did on the same errand. The other, the
Rev. Thomas Law, Organizing Secretary of the Free Church
Federation, has been in Wales for some time, and had excellent opportunities of studying the question in various
districts in South Wales. I think I am justified in saying
that both Mr. Law and Gipsy Smith are absolutely at one
with me in the conclusions which I embodied in my report
to *The Daily Chronicle* of Tuesday. During my stay in
Wales I had the advantage of hearing the opinions of Principal Edwards and of Commissioner Nicol, of the Salvation
Army, and of several other ministers who have been actively
engaged in Christian service in the districts where the revival has taken place. After my return I had a long con-
sultation with Mr. Bramwell Booth, who knows the district
well, and who had visited Cardiff on Saturday, where he
met members of his staff from all parts of South Wales, for
the express purpose of ascertaining on the spot what was
the exact significance of the revival. I also saw the special
emissary despatched by the Rev. F. B. Meyer for the purpose of spying out the land, and heard from him the impres-
sion produced on his mind by what he had seen and heard.
The reports in the two local newspapers, which occasionally
fill five columns and always fill two or three, also supplied ad-
ditional confirmatory evidence as to the grip which the movement has taken on the Welsh. I attended three protracted
meetings on the Sunday, and I had an hour with Mr. Evan
Roberts. I am careful to particularize all my sources of
information in order that my readers may know exactly

what data I have to go upon in drawing up this report for
the readers of *The Christian World*. My own experience
may be of the slightest, and my visit was wonderfully brief.
But I think that I may claim that there are few Free Churchmen in the United Kingdom who would not admit that I
could not possibly have had more expert advisers or dispas-
sionate witnesses than the persons whom I have named.
Nor do I think that any one of them would demur in the
least to any statement of fact or broad deduction from the
facts which will be found in this article. Had time permitted I would have gladly submitted my report to each
and all of them in proofs, nor do I think that they would
have made any material alteration.

This being so, I take it that the Christian churches in
England may accept it as now being absolutely beyond all
serious dispute that the revival in South Wales is a very
real and a very genuine thing. That there may have been
here and there instances of unwisdom and of extravagance
is possible. They have been very few and unimportant.
The Welsh are an emotional race, and they are apt to
demonstrate their feelings more effusively than phlegmatic
Saxons. But I certainly saw nothing of that kind that
might not be paralleled in mission services in England.
The fact is, there has been so little handle given to the
enemy who ever is hungering for occasion to blaspheme,
that the revival, so far, lacks that one great testimony in its
favor which all good causes have in the furious abuse of
those who may compendiously and picturesquely be described as the staff-officers of the devil.   "Woe unto you,
when all men shall speak well of you !" was true of revivals
as of anything else. The revival has, so far, had little of
that cause for rejoicing that is supplied by persecution and
abuse. The testimony in its favor is almost wearisomely
monotonous. Magistrates and policemen, journalists and

employers of labor, Salvationists and ordained ministers,
all say the same thing, to wit, that the revival is working
mightily for good wherever it has broken out.

Of course, the Doubting Thomases of the land will shake
their sceptical heads, and, when convinced against their will
that the revival is bearing good fruit, will ask whether it
will last.   To which I do not hesitate to reply that some of
its fruits will last as long as the human soul endures.   That
a good deal of the seed which, having fallen on stony
ground, has sprung up speedily will presently wither away
is a matter of course.   It was so when the Parable of the
Sower was spoken; it is so to-day.   But the cavilers forget
that it is a better thing for seed to spring up, even if it does
wither, than for it never to spring up at all.   Even if the
farmer does not get the full corn in the ear, the green stalk
with its succulent leaves will make capital fodder for his
stock.   Most of the seed sown at times when we hear of no
showers of blessings to fertilize the soil never springs up at
all.   Little as the cavilers about the evanescent nature of
revivals realize it, they are appealing to one of the most
antiquated notions of a narrow orthodoxy.   Those who imagine that the only object of the Christian gospel is to save
a man's soul from the everlasting burnings may reasonably
object that a revival is of no good if, after having roused
the sinner, it does not keep him soundly saved until the
hour and article of death.   It is in that case very much like
taking out an insurance policy and letting it lapse by for-
getting to pay the premiums regularly till death.   But there
are very few who regard conversion as an insurance policy
against hell-fire.   Hence every single day or week or month
or year is all to the good.   It is, of course, best of all when
a consecrated life is crowned by a triumphant death.   But
it is not a bad thing—on the contrary, it is a very good
thing—to raise human lives to a higher moral level for a

comparatively short period, even if after that time they all
slide back.   It is better to have lived well for a year than
never to have been above the mire at all.   As a matter of
fact, most of the best men of the older generation in Wales
to-day were brought in when quite youths in the great
revival of 1859.

So far as I could discover, the movement is in very good
hands—so far as it is in any hands at all save those of the
invisible Spirit to which all the revivalists constantly appeal.
Never was there a religious movement so little indebted to
the guiding brain of its leaders.   It seems to be going "on
its own."   There is no commanding human genius inspiring the advance.   Ministers, each in his own church,
open the meetings.   But when once they are started they
"obey the Spirit."   It reminds one of the Quakers in more
ways than one.   In the seventeenth century the Friends
were the revivalists of the time.   With the exception of the
singing, they would feel themselves thoroughly at home in
South Wales to-day.   In most missions tune is everything.
In South Wales the leading rôle is taken by the third Person
of the Trinity.   So jealous are they of quenching the Spirit
that the Tory daily paper—just think of it—the organ of
the Established Church and ease and order and all the rest
of the conventions—actually fumed and fretted because at
one meeting some persons who were giving unbridled rein to
their spiritual impulses, to the annoyance of the whole congregation, were asked to restrain their exuberance of their
demonstrations !   If this thing goes on we shall see *The
Times* and *The Guardian* reproving General Booth for
endeavoring to repress the excesses of excitement at all-
night meetings.

I have said that the early Friends would be at home in
the Welsh valleys with the exception of the singing.   It is a
great exception.   For the special note of the revival is that

the gospel message is being sung rather than preached.
And such singing ! The whole congregation sing—as if
they were making melody in their hearts to the Lord. The
sermon is a poor thing compared with the psalm and hymn
and spiritual song. The Welsh have hymns of their own,
which were strange to me. I have no musical ear, but the
rhythm and the cadence of some of these Welsh tunes linger
in my memory as the murmur of the wave in the convolu-
tions of the shell. There is one beginning with the Welsh
equivalent for " Holy breezes," which was a great favorite ;
and so is another which gives thanks to the all-merciful God
for remembering us poor creatures who are as the dust
of the earth. But most of them were the old familiar
hymns of every mission service. Occasionally they sang
"Lead, kindly Light," but much more frequently " Jesus,
lover of my soul," "I need thee every hour," "Lord, I
hear of showers of blessings," all in Welsh, of course,
although very often, after singing the chorus over and over
again in Welsh, they would sing it once or twice in English.
Among the solos there was Mr. Sankey's "Ninety and
nine," which, although turned out of the revised Methodist
Hymn Book, is written on the hearts of the Welsh. " Jesus
of Nazareth passes by " is another favorite solo. The only
new song taken over from the Torrey and Alexander Mission was sung over and over again :

> Tell mother I 'll be there
> In answer to her prayer,
> This message, blessed Saviour, to her bear.
> Tell mother I 'll be there,
> Heaven's joys with her to share,
> Oh, tell my darling mother I 'll be there.

In the Gospel the Prodigal Son comes back to his father.
It is perhaps an indication of the swing of the slow pendu-

lum back to the days of the matriarchate that in Wales to-
day the father takes a back seat. It is the mother who is
always to the front.

Nor is that the only welcome indication of the toppling of
the hateful and unchristian ascendancy of the male. The
old objection of many of the Welsh churches to the equal
ministry of women has gone by the board. The Singing
Sisters who surround Mr. Evan Roberts are as indispensable
as Mr. Sankey was to Mr. Moody. Women pray, sing,
testify and speak as freely as men—no one daring to make
them afraid. The Salvation Army has not labored in vain.

There is no inquiry room, no penitent form. The
wrestle with unbelief, the combat with the evil one for the
soul of the convicted sinner, goes on in the midst of the
people. It is all intensely dramatic; sometimes unspeak-
ably tragic; at other times full of exultant triumph. Mr.
Evan Roberts, toward the close of the meeting, asks all who
from their hearts believe and confess their Saviour to rise.
At the meetings at which I was present nearly everybody
was standing. Then for the sitting remnant the storm of
prayer rises to the mercy seat. When one after another
rises to his feet, glad strains of jubilant song burst from the
watching multitude. No one has a hymn-book; no one
gives out a hymn. The congregation seems moved by a
simultaneous impulse. It is all very wonderful, sometimes
almost eery in its suggestiveness of the presence of Another
whom no eye can see, but who moves on the wings of the
wind.

Who can say to what this thing may not grow? Who
can put bounds to the flood of awakened enthusiasm? One
thing is certain—no one could wish to erect a barrier save
those who do not love their fellow men.

The report which I wrote for *The Daily Chronicle* was
written for the general public, who are comparatively indifferent to the spiritual side of the revival, but who regard its
social and psychological aspects with a mild degree of
interest.

From "The Daily Chronicle"
December 13th.

As springtime precedes summer, and seed-time harvest,
so every great onward step in the social and political progress of Great Britain has ever been preceded by a national
revival of religion. The sequence is as unmistakable as it
is invariable. It was as constant when England was Cath-
olic as it has been since the Reformation.

Hence it is not necessary to be evangelical, Christian, or
even religious, to regard with keen interest every stirring of
popular enthusiasm that takes the familiar form of a revival.
Men may despise it, hate it, or fear it, but there is no mis-
taking its significance. It is the precursor of progress, the
herald of advance. It may as evanescent as the blossom
of the orchard, but without it there would be no fruit.

The question, therefore, which I set out to South Wales
to discuss with those who are in the midst of what is called
The Welsh Revival was whether this popular stir and wide-
spread awakening might be regarded as the forerunner of a
great national—nay, possibly of a still wider—movement,
which might bring in its wake social and political changes
profoundly improving the condition of the human race.

Nor would I like to venture to predict how long or how
short a time it will be before that heading in its turn will
have to give way to the simple title of "The Revival,"
which will be neither in the West alone, nor in the East, but
which will spread over the whole land as the waters cover
the face of the mighty deep. Of course, the signs of the

times may be misleading, and that which seems most probable may never happen. But writing to-day in the midst of it all, I would say with all earnestness, "Look out!"

"The British Empire," as Admiral Fisher is never tired of repeating, "floats upon the British navy." But the British navy steams on Welsh coal. The driving force of all our battleships is hewn from the mines of these Welsh valleys by the men amongst whom this remarkable religious awakening has taken place. On Sunday morning, as the slow train crawled down the gloomy valleys—for there was the mirk of coming snow in the air, and there was no sun in the sky—I could not avoid the obvious and insistent suggestion of the thought that Welsh religious enthusiasm may be destined to impart as compelling an impulse to the churches of the world as Welsh coal supplies to its navies.

Nor was the force of the suggestion weakened when, after attending three prolonged services at Mardy, a village of 5,000 inhabitants, lying on the other side of Pontypridd, I found the flame of Welsh religious enthusiasm as smokeless as its coal. There are no advertisements, no brass bands, no posters, no huge tents. All the paraphernalia of the got-up job are conspicuous by their absence.

Neither is there any organization, nor is there a director, at least none that is visible to the human eye. In the crowded chapels they even dispense with instrumental music. On Sunday night no note issued from the organ pipes. There was no need of instruments, for in and around and above and beneath surged the all-pervading thrill and throb of a multitude praying, and singing as they prayed.

The vast congregations were as soberly sane, as orderly, and at least as reverent as any congregation I ever saw beneath the dome of St. Paul's, when I used to go to hear Canon Liddon, the Chrysostom of the English pulpit. But it was aflame with a passionate religious enthusiasm, the like of which I have never seen in St. Paul's. Tier above tier, from the crowded aisles to the loftiest gallery, sat or stood, as necessity dictated, eager hundreds of serious men and thoughtful women, their eyes riveted upon the platform or upon whatever other part of the building was the storm center of the meeting.

There was absolutely nothing wild, violent, hysterical, unless it be hysterical for the laboring breast to heave with sobbing that cannot be repressed, and the throat to choke with emotion as a sense of the awful horror and shame of a wasted life suddenly bursts upon the soul. On all sides there was the solemn gladness of men and women upon whose eyes has dawned the splendor of a new day, the foretaste of whose glories they are enjoying in the quickened sense of human fellowship and a keen, glad zest added to their own lives.

The most thoroughgoing materialist who resolutely and forever rejects as inconceivable the existence of the soul in man, and to whom " the universe is but the infinite empty eye-socket of a dead God," could not fail to be impressed by the pathetic sincerity of these men ; nor, if he were just, could he refuse to recognize that out of their faith in the creed which he has rejected they have drawn, and are drawing, a motive power that makes for righteousness, and not only for righteousness, but for the joy of living, that he would be powerless to give them.

Employers tell me that the quality of the work the miners are putting in has improved. Waste is less, men go to their daily toil with a new spirit of gladness in their labor. In the long, dim galleries of the mine, where once the hauliers swore at their ponies in Welshified English terms of blasphemy, there is now but to be heard the haunting melody of the revival music. The pit ponies, like the American mules, having been driven by oaths and curses since they first bore the yoke, are being retrained to do their work without the incentive of profanity.

There is less drinking, less idleness, less gambling. Men record with almost incredulous amazement how one football player after another has foresworn cards and drink and the gladiatorial games, and is living a sober and godly life, putting his energy into the revival. More wonderful still, and almost incredible to those who know how journalism lives and thrives upon gambling, and how Toryism is broadbased upon the drinking habits of the people, the Tory daily paper of South Wales has devoted its columns day after day to reporting and defending the movement which declares war to the death against both gambling and drink.

How came this strange uplift of the earnestness of a whole community? Who can say? The wind bloweth where it listeth. Some tell you one thing, some another. All agree that it began some few months ago in Cardiganshire, eddied hither and thither, spreading like fire from valley to valley, until, as one observer said to me, "Wherever it came from, or however it began, all South Wales to-day is in a flame."

One report says that the first outward and visible sign that there was a new power and spirit among the people was witnessed at a meeting in a country chapel in Cardiganshire. The preacher, after an earnest appeal to the unconverted, besought those of his hearers whose hearts were moved within them to testify before the congregation their decision to serve the Lord. A long and painful pause followed. Again came the solemn appeal. Again the embarrassing silence.

But it was broken after a pause by the rising of a girl, a young Welsh woman, who with trembling accents spoke up and said, "If no one else will, then I must say that I do

love my Lord Jesus Christ with all my heart." The ice
was broken. One after another stood up and made public
confessions with tears and thanksgiving.

So it began. So it is going on. " If no one else, then I
must." It is " Here am I : send me ! " This public self-
consecration, this definite and decisive avowal of a determi-
nation to put under their feet their dead past of vice and sin
and indifference, and to reach out toward a higher ideal of
human existence, is going on everywhere in South Wales.
Nor, if we think of it sanely and look at it in the right per-
spective, is there a nobler spectacle appealing more directly
to the highest instincts of our nature to be seen in all the
world to-day.

At Mardy, where I spent Sunday, the miners are volun-
tarily taxing themselves this year three-halfpence in the
pound of their weekly wages to build an institute, public
hall, library, and reading-room. By their express request
the money is deducted from their wages on pay-day. They
have created a library of 2,000 books, capitally selected and
well used. They have about half-a-dozen chapels and
churches, a cooperative society, and the usual appliances of
civilization. They have every outward and visible sign of
industrial prosperity. It is a mining village pure and
simple, industrial democracy in its nakedest primitive form.

In this village I attended three meetings on Sunday—two
and a half hours in the morning, two and a half hours in
the afternoon, and two hours at night, when I had to leave
to catch the train. At all these meetings the same kind of
thing went on—the same kind of congregations assembled,
the same strained, intense emotion was manifest. Aisles
were crowded. Pulpit stairs were packed, and—*mirabile
dictu !*—two-thirds of the congregation were men, and at
least one-half young men.

" There," said one," is the hope and the glory of the

movement." Here and there is a gray head. But the majority of the congregation were stalwart young miners, who
gave the meeting all the fervor and swing and enthusiasm
of youth. The revival had been going on in Mardy for a
fortnight. All the churches had been holding services every
night with great results. At the Baptist church they had to
report the addition of nearly fifty members, fifty were waiting for baptism, thirty-five backsliders had been re-
claimed.

In Mardy the fortnight's services had resulted in five hundred conversions. And this, be it noted, when each place
of worship was going "on its own." Mr. Evan Roberts,
the so-called boy preacher of the revival, and his singing
sisterhood did not reach Mardy until the Sunday of my
visit.

I have called Evan Roberts the so-called boy preacher,
because he is neither a boy nor a preacher. He is a tall,
graceful, good-looking young man of twenty-six, with a
pleading eye and a most winsome smile. If he is a boy, he
is a six-foot boy, and six-footers are usually past their boy-
hood. As he is not a boy, neither is he a preacher. He
talks simply, unaffectedly, earnestly, now and then, but he
makes no sermons, and preaching is emphatically not the
note of this revival in the West. If it has been by the
foolishness of preaching men have been saved heretofore,
that agency seems as if it were destined to take a back seat
in the present movement.

The revival is borne along upon billowing waves of sacred
song. It is to other revivals what the Italian opera is to the
ordinary theater. It is the singing, not the preaching, that
is the instrument which is most efficacious in striking the
hearts of men. In this respect these services in the Welsh
chapel reminded me strangely of the beautiful liturgical
services of the Greek Church, notably in St. Isaac of St.

Petersburg on Easter morn, and in the receptions of the pilgrim at the Troitski Monastery, near Moscow.

The most extraordinary thing about the meetings which I attended was the extent to which they were absolutely without any human direction or leadership. " We must obey the Spirit," is the watchword of Evan Roberts, and he is as obedient as the humblest of his followers. The meetings open—after any amount of preliminary singing, while the congregation is assembling—by the reading of a chapter or a psalm. Then it is go-as-you-please for two hours or more.

And the amazing thing is that it does go and does not get entangled in what might seem to be inevitable confusion. Three-fourths of the meeting consist of singing. No one uses a hymn-book. No one gives out a hymn. The last person to control the meeting in any way is Mr. Evan Roberts. People pray and sing, give testimony, exhort as the Spirit moves them. As a study of the psychology of crowds, I have seen nothing like it. You feel that the thousand or fifteen hundred persons before you have become merged into one myriad-headed but single-souled personality.

You can watch what they call the influence of the power of the Spirit playing over the crowded congregation as an eddying wind plays over the surface of a pond. If any one carried away by his feelings prays too long, or if any one when speaking fails to touch the right note, some one—it may be anybody—commences to sing. For a moment there is a hesitation as if the meeting were in doubt as to its decision, whether to hear the speaker, or to continue to join in the prayer, or whether to sing. If it decides to hear and to pray, the singing dies away. If, on the other hand, as it usually happens, the people decide to sing, the chorus swells in volume until it drowns all other sound.

A very remarkable instance of this abandonment of the

meeting to the spontaneous impulse, not merely of those within the walls, but of those crowded outside, who were unable to get in, occurred on Sunday night. Twice the order of proceeding, if order it can be called, was altered by the crowd outside, who, being moved by some mysterious impulse, started a hymn on their own account, which was at once taken up by the congregation within. On one of these occasions Evan Roberts was addressing the meeting. He at once gave way, and the singing became general.

The prayers are largely autobiographical, and some of them intensely dramatic. On one occasion an impassioned and moving appeal to the Deity was accompanied throughout by an exquisitely rendered hymn, sung by three of the Singing Sisters. It was like the undertone of the orchestra when some leading singer is holding the house.

The Singing Sisters—there are five of them, one, Mme. Morgan, who was a professional singer—are as conspicuous figures in the movement as Evan Roberts himself. Some of their solos are wonders of dramatic and musical appeal. Nor is the effect lessened by the fact that the singers, like the speakers, sometimes break down in sobs and tears. The meeting always breaks out into a passionate and consoling song, until the soloist, having recovered her breath, rises from her knees and resumes her song.

The praying and singing are both wonderful, but more impressive than either are the breaks which occur when utterance can no more, and the sobbing in the silence momentarily heard is drowned in a tempest of melody. No need for an organ. The assembly was its own organ as a thousand sorrowing or rejoicing hearts found expression in the sacred psalmody of their native hills.

Repentance, open confession, intercessory prayer, and, above all else, this marvelous musical liturgy—a liturgy unwritten but heartfelt, a mighty chorus rising like the thunder of the surge on a rock-bound shore, ever and anon broken by the flute-like note of the Singing Sisters, whose melody was as sweet and as spontaneous as the music of the throstle in the grove or the lark in the sky. And all this vast, quivering, throbbing, singing, praying, exultant multitude intensely conscious of the all-pervading influence of some invisible reality—now for the first time moving palpable though not tangible in their midst.

They called it the Spirit of God. Those who have not witnessed it may call it what they will; I am inclined to agree with those on the spot. For man, being, according to the orthodox, evil, can do no good thing of himself, so, as Cardinal Manning used to say, "Wherever you behold a good thing, there you see the working of the Holy Ghost." And the revival, as I saw it, was emphatically a good thing.

CHAPTER IV

EVAN ROBERTS

The revival in South Wales is not the work of any one man or of any number of men, but the most conspicuous figure in this strange religious awakening is undoubtedly that of the young Welsh collier-student, Mr. Evan Roberts. Until last November no one had heard of him. To-day his name is on every tongue in Wales, and everywhere in all the land people are asking what manner of man this new evangelist may be.

Mr. Evan Roberts is a tall, graceful young man of twenty-six, who, until last year, was at work as a collier in the Broadoak Colliery, Loughor, a Welsh village near which an express train was wrecked a few months ago, with great loss of life. He is the son of Methodist parents, and attended the Movrah Methodist Chapel in Loughor. Like many Welshmen, he is a poet, and contributed many fine verses to the Golofn Gymraag in *The Cardiff Times* under the name of "Bwlchydd." He was always of a pious disposition, but according to his own account, although he was a church member and a worker in the Sunday-school, he was not a Christian until little more than fifteen months ago. His own words at Trecynon, on November 14th, were as follows :

Some people had said he was a Methodist. He did not know what he was. Sectarianism melted in the fire of the Holy Spirit, and all men who believed became one happy family. For years he was a faithful member of the church,

48

a zealous worker, and a free giver. But he had recently discovered that he was not a Christian, and there were thousands like him. It was only since he had made that' discovery that a new light had come into his life. That same light was shining upon all men if they would but open their eyes and their hearts.

How did he make that discovery? Various accounts have been given of the awakening of Evan Roberts. According to one account, he was present at an address delivered by the Rev. F. B. Meyer at a religious Convention in August, 1903, when a pledge was given by several present, including Roberts, that they would spend a whole day every month praying for a revival. According to Mr. Roberts' own account, he seems to have been chiefly exercised in his devotions by a melancholy conviction of the failure of Christianity. He was then living at Loughor, working in the mine and spending his leisure in studying for the ministry. He used to take his Bible down the mine, and while at work would put it away in some convenient hole or nook near his working place, ready to his hand when He could snatch a moment or two to scan its beloved pages. A serious explosion occurred one day. The future Welsh revivalist escaped practically unhurt, but the leaves of his Bible were scorched by the fiery blast.

It was during the latter months of his stay at Loughor, before he went to the preparatory school or college at Newcastle Emlyn, that the light dawned upon him in the privacy of his own room. He seems to have been very fervent in prayer. A Mr. Davies, a Newport Baptist, is the authority for the statement that Roberts was turned out of his lodgings by his landlady, who thought that in his enthusiasm he was possessed or somewhat mad. He spent hours praying and preaching in his rooms, until the lady became afraid of him and asked him to leave. The following narrative I had from his own lips when I met him at tea on Sunday afternoon at Mardy. I asked him—

"Can you tell me how you began to take to this work?"

"Oh, yes, that I will," said Mr. Roberts, "if you wish to hear of it. For a long, long time I was much troubled in my soul and my heart by thinking over the failure of Christianity. Oh, it seemed such a failure—such a failure—and I prayed and prayed, but nothing seemed to give me any relief! But one night, after I had been in great distress praying about this, I went to sleep, and at one o'clock in the morning suddenly I was waked up out of my sleep, and I found myself, with unspeakable joy and awe, in the very presence of Almighty God. And for the space of four hours I was privileged to speak face to face with him as a man speaks face to face with a friend. At five o'clock it seemed to me as if I again returned to earth."[1]

"Were you not dreaming?" I asked.

"No, I was wide awake. And it was not only that morning, but every morning for three or four months. Always I enjoyed four hours of that wonderful communion with God. I cannot describe it. I felt it, and it seemed to

---

[1] Mr. J. Addington Symonds records a somewhat similar experience when under chloroform. He says: "I thought that I was near death, when suddenly my soul became aware of God, who was manifestly dealing with me, handling me, so to speak, in an intense personal present reality. I felt him streaming in like light upon me. I cannot describe the ecstasy I felt." When the effect of the anæsthetic faded, he longed for death, rather than to lose "that long dateless ecstasy of vision" in which he felt "the very God in all purity and tenderness and truth and absolute love." He adds: "The question remains, is it possible that the inner sense of reality which succeeded when my flesh was dead to impressions from without to the ordinary sense of physical relations was not a delusion but an actual experience? Is it possible that I in that moment felt what some of the saints have said they always felt, the undemonstrable but irrefragable certainty of God?"—*Symonds's works, cited by James*, p. 392.

See also the experiences of Madame Guyon: "It seemed to me that God came at the precise time and woke me from sleep in order that I might enjoy him."—*Ib.*, p. 277.

change all my nature, and I saw things in a different light, and I knew that God was going to work in the land, and not this land only, but in all the world." [1]

"Excuse me," I said, "but, as an old interviewer, may I ask if, when the mystic ecstasy passed, you put on paper all that you remembered of these times of communion?"

"No, I wrote nothing at all," [2] said Mr. Roberts. "It went on all the time until I had to go to Newcastle Emlyn to the college to prepare for the ministry. I dreaded to go, for fear I should lose these four hours with God every morning. But I had to go, and it happened as I feared. For a whole month he came no more, and I was in darkness. And my heart became as a stone. Even the sight of the cross brought no tears to my eyes. So it continued until, to my great joy, he returned to me, and I had again

---

[1] This mystic vision, which enables a man to comprehend the secret of God in the creation and ordering of the universe, was common to all the great saints, and also to one not usually classed as a saint, Walt Whitman. George Fox was so confident that the nature and virtues of all things had been opened to him by the Lord that he actually contemplated practising physic for the good of mankind. Ignatius Loyola, on the steps of the choir of the Dominican church, saw in a distinct manner the plan of Divine Wisdom in the creation of the world. St. Teresa says that it was granted to her one day to perceive in one instant how all things are seen and contained in God. Jacob Boehme, in one quarter of a day in trance, saw and knew the being of all things. Whitman wrote:—

"I mind how once we (my soul and I) lay, such a transparent summer morning,
Swiftly arose to spread around me the peace and knowledge
That pass all the argument of the earth;
And I know that the hand of God is the promise of my own;
And I know that the Spirit of God is the brother of my own,
And that all the men ever born are also my brothers, and the women my sisters and lovers,
And that a kelson of the creation is love."—*Ib.*, p. 396.

[2] Professor James writing on the mystical absorption of the Sufis into God says: "The incommunicableness of the transport is the key-note of all mysticism. Mystical truth exists for the individual who has the transport, but for no one else."—*Symond's works, etc.*, p. 404.

the glorious communion. And he said I must go and
speak to my people in my own village. But I did not go.
I did not feel as if I could go to speak to my own people."

"May I ask," I said, "if he of whom you speak appeared to you as Jesus Christ?"

"No," said Mr. Roberts, "not so; it was the personal
God, not as Jesus."

"As God the Father Almighty?" I said.

"Yes," said Mr. Roberts, "and the Holy Spirit."[1]

"Pardon me," I said, "but I interrupted you. Pray go
on."

"I did not go to my people, but I was troubled and ill at
ease. And one Sunday, as I sat in the chapel, I could not
fix my mind upon the service, for always before my eyes I
saw, as in a vision, the schoolroom in my own village.
And there, sitting in rows before me, I saw my old com-
panions and all the young people, and I saw myself addressing them. I shook my head impatiently, and strove to
drive away this vision, but it always came back. And I
heard a voice in my inward ear as plain as anything, saying, 'Go and speak to these people.' And for a long time
I would not. But the pressure became greater and greater,
and I could hear nothing of the sermon. Then at last I
could resist no longer, and I said, 'Well, Lord, if it is thy
will, I will go.' Then instantly the vision vanished, and
the whole chapel became filled with light so dazzling
that I could faintly see the minister in the pulpit, and

[1] George Fox used to converse with Jesus Christ; but St. Teresa,
like Evan Roberts, spoke with God. She says: "God establishes
himself in the interior of the soul in such a way that when she returns
to herself it is wholly impossible for her to doubt that she has been in
God and God in her. This truth remained so strongly impressed on
her that even though many years should pass without the condition returning, she can neither forget the favor she received nor doubt of the
reality."—*Symond's works, etc.*, p. 409.

between him and me the glory as the light of the sun in heaven." [1]

"And then you went home?"

"No; I went to my tutor, and told him all things, and asked him if he believed that it was of God or of the devil? And he said the devil does not put good thoughts into the mind. I must go and obey the heavenly vision. So I went back to my own village, and I saw my own minister, and him also I told. And he said that I might try and see what I could do, but that the ground was stony, and the task would be hard."

"Did you find it so?"

"I asked the young people to come together, for I wanted to talk to them. They came, and I stood up to talk to them, and, behold, it was even as I had seen it in the church at Newcastle Emlyn. The young people sat as I had seen them sitting, all together in rows before me, and I was speaking to them even as it had been shown to me. At first they did not seem inclined to listen; but I went on, and at last the power of the Spirit came down, and six came out for Jesus. But I was not satisfied. 'O Lord,' I said, 'give me six more—I must have six more!' And we prayed together. At last the seventh came, and then the eighth and the ninth together, and after a time the tenth, and then the eleventh, and last of all came the twelfth also. But no more. And they saw that the Lord had given me the second six, and they began to believe in the power of prayer."

[1] This, again, is one of the most familiar phenomena of ecstasy. Professor James says: "There is one form of sensory automatism which possibly deserves special notice on account of its frequency. I refer to hallucinatory or pseudo-hallucinatory luminous phenomena, photisms, to use the term of the psychologists. St. Paul's blinding heavenly vision seems to have been a phenomenon of this order. So does Constantine's cross in the sky. Colonel Gardner sees a blazing light. Finney says, 'A light perfectly ineffable shone in my soul.'" —*Symond's works, etc.,* p. 252.

"Then after that you went on?"

"First I tried to speak to some other young people in another church, and asked them to come. But the news had gone out, and the old people said, 'May we not come too?' And I could not refuse them. So they came, and they kept on coming now here, now there, all the time, and I have never had time to go back to college."

Not much chance, indeed, at present. Three meetings every day, lasting, with breaks for meals, from 10 A. M. till 12 P. M., and sometimes later, leave scant leisure for studying elsewhere than in the hearts and souls of men. If only his body will hold out, and his nervous system does not give way, he will have time to study hereafter. At present he has other work in hand.

The story that is told in the papers pieces out Mr. Roberts' own narrative. According to the Rev. Seth Joshua, a mission from the New Quay Christian Endeavor Society came to Newcastle Emlyn, and it was at one of their meetings that Evan Roberts first showed his marvelous power in prayer.

Whatever truth there may be in this link in the chain, there is no doubt that Mr. Evan Roberts began to preach and to pray at the Movrah Methodist Church in Loughor about the beginning of November. The most extraordinary results followed. The whole community was shaken. Meetings were kept up till half-past four, and then at six the villagers would be wakened by the tramp of the crowds going to the early morning prayer-meetings. His energy seemed inexhaustible. In those early days, said a writer in *The South Wales Daily News* (November 14th):

Roberts does not call his hearers to repentance, but speaks of having been called to fulfil the words of the prophet Joel: "Your old men shall dream dreams, your young men shall see visions." He tells the audience that he is speaking under the influence of the Holy Spirit, and he describes what he sees, and it strikes some of the congregation that he is unfathoming unconsciously some of the mysteries of the Book of Revelation. His words have a remarkable effect. He does not speak much, but invites the congregation to sing, or pray, or read the Scripture as the Spirit moves them.

Mr. Roberts frequently describes visions that had appeared to him at prayer. For instance:

He said that when he was before the throne of grace he saw appearing before him a key. He did not understand the meaning of this sign. Just then, however, three members of the congregation rose to their feet and said that they had been converted. " My vision is explained," said Mr. Roberts, ecstatically; " it was the key by which God opened your hearts."

On another occasion he reverted to his experiences at Newcastle Emlyn, and told them of another vision. He said (*The South Wales Daily News*, November 19th):

It was a few Sundays ago at Newcastle Emlyn. For days he had been brooding over the apparent failure of modern Christian agencies; and he felt wounded in the spirit that the Church of God should so often be attacked. While in this Slough of Despond he walked in the garden. It was about 4 P. M. Suddenly, in the hedge on his left, he saw a face full of scorn, hatred and derision, and heard a laugh as of defiance. It was the prince of this world, who exulted in his despondency. Then there suddenly appeared another figure, gloriously arrayed in white, bearing in hand a flaming sword borne aloft. The sword fell athwart the first figure, and it instantly disappeared. He could not see the face of the sword-bearer. " Do you not see the moral ? " queried the missioner, with face beaming with delight. " Is it not that the Church of Christ is to be triumphant ? "

Significant glances passed between many people in the congregation. Visions? What does the man mean? He is speaking in parables. So far he has been a sane speaker, and with no trace about him of the fanatic. He cannot mean to convey that ——. But we are speedily undeceived. "I told the Rev. Evan Phillips of what I had seen, and he answered me that in the state of despondency I was in I might easily have imagined the vision. But "—with strong emphasis—"I know what I saw. It was a distinct vision. There was no mistake. And, full of the promise which that vision conveyed, I went to Loughor, and from Loughor to Aberdare, and from Aberdare to Pontycymmer. And what do I see? The promise literally fulfilled. The sword is descending on all hands, and Satan is put to flight. Amen."

*Roberts'
preaching* It has been said that Mr. Roberts never preaches. He does, however, or rather he did at the beginning of his career deliver long addresses, which were simple, direct Gospel appeals. Joyousness was the note of all his discourse, the joyousness of a junior partner conscious that his Senior is with him and is entrusting him with a most responsible mission.

He exclaimed once: "Oh, if you only saw Christ, you would love him! How can I repay him for the privilege of going through Wales to proclaim his love?"

At Pyle, November 21, speaking of the work that is being done, Mr. Roberts joyously clapped his hands and shouted, "Aha, aha," but remarked that this sort of thing could not go on forever—this fever-heat could not be kept going long; but let them keep it going as long as they could; let them keep it going with a swing (which he illustrated with a swing of his right arm), to raise the churches to a higher level, and then they could "settle down to business." At the end of November he gave it as his conviction that one hundred thousand souls would be won before the end of the revival in Wales. In December he said: "At one time I said I would be satisfied with one hundred thousand converts and then would be willing to die, but now I want the whole world."

Again he says: "Isn't it all wonderful how the Spirit responds? It is not me—it is the Spirit, the Spirit."

To describe the address that follows as a sermon would be a misnomer. He is buoyant, joyous, almost bubbling over with merriment. It is "the joy of Christ," he explains, "and you can laugh—yes, laugh out of sheer joy at the throne of grace."

Yet he always shrinks modestly from claiming any of the results that follow his mission; sometimes he declines to let his movements be announced. "People must not rely upon me." This is his constant cry. "I have nothing for them. They must rely upon Him who alone can minister to their needs."

When I talked with him, he said:

"The movement is not of me, it is of God. I would not dare to try to direct it. Obey the Spirit, that is our word in everything. It is the Spirit alone which is leading us in our meetings and in all that is done."

"You do not preach, or teach, or control the meetings?"

"Why should I teach when the Spirit is teaching? What need have these people to be told that they are sinners? What they need is salvation. Do they not know it? It is not knowledge that they lack, but decision—action. And why should I control the meetings? The meetings control themselves, or rather the Spirit that is in them controls them."

"You find the ministry of the Singing Sisters useful?"

"Most useful. They go with me wherever I go. I never part from them without feeling that something is absent if they are not there. The singing is very important,

but not everything. No. The public confession is also important—more so than the speaking. True, I talk to them
a little. But the meetings go of themselves."

"Do you propose to go to England?"

"No. To North Wales next. They say North Wales is
stony cold, but I believe the Holy Spirit will work there
also. Oh, yes, God will move North Wales also."

All his movements are governed by the answers he re-
ceives to prayer. "Will you go to Cardiff?" they asked
him. He paused, and then replied in the negative, the answer to his thought-prayer having been almost instantaneous.
He usually speaks in Welsh, but he can speak English,
although not with the beauty and polish of his native
tongue. The newspapers publish translated scraps rather
than reports of his remarks. Here are a few sentences:

"Whilst sect was fighting against sect the devil was clap-
ping his hands with glee, and encouraging the fight. Let
all people be one, with one object—the salvation of sinners.
Men refused to accept the gospel and confess because, they
said, of the gloom and uncertainty of the future. They
looked to the future without having opened their eyes to the
infinite glories of the present."

"All must obey," he declares, "all must work. There
is no room in the church for idlers. Are you an idler?
Then your place is outside." "Be as simple in your wor-
shiping as possible, the simpler the better. There is no
need to shout," he went on, "and no one need be ashamed
to confess Christ."

He dwells sometimes on the sufferings of Christ until he
falls prone, sobs choking his utterance. While absolutely
tolerant of all manifestations of the Spirit, he is stern to
check any disorder. At Ferndale, where some persons had
been disturbing the meeting by exuberant and unseemly
noises, he said: "He who would walk with God must

come to his house in a spirit of prayer, of humility, of awe. Joy is permissible in the house, but it must be sanctified joy. For think of the majesty of the Divine Person. Father— yes, a Father truly, but we must be even as little children, in humility, remembering that we are sinners. We can, we are taught to entreat for the descent of the Spirit, but beware lest the entreaty becomes a rude, imperious command. If we truly walk with God, there can be no disorder, no indecency."

On another occasion he pleaded for a Service of Silence, to convince the world that the power at work in those gatherings was the power of the Holy Spirit, not that of man. "Let us have five minutes of absolutely silent prayers"—an effective reversion to the practice of the Society of Friends.

His method of conducting a meeting is to allow it to conduct itself. But he usually contrives to expound his four principles, and to summon his hearers to make public confession.

The following is the best report which I have been able to piece together after a diligent study of all the papers published since the revival began. He addresses his audience thus :

Do you desire an outpouring of the Holy Spirit ?
Very well. Four conditions must be observed. They are essential.

(1) Is there any sin in your past life that you have not confessed to God? On your knees at once. Your past must be at peace.

(2) Is there anything in your life that is doubtful ? Anything you cannot decide whether it is good or evil ? Away with it ! There must not be !

(3) Obey the Spirit.

(4) Confess Christ publicly before men."

After the meeting has gone on for some time Roberts proceeds to put his testing questions. I quote the description given by *The South Wales Daily News* on December 14:

The missioner is now at work. He has three questions to put. He has been told, commanded, imperatively commanded, to put the questions, and he dare not disobey. He could never sleep if he didn't put them.

(1) "Will every member of a Christian Church stand up?"

There is immediate response. Few, very few, are sitting. But a second later we are surprised by the announcement from the gallery that some are standing who are not members. "Come, friends," exclaims the missioner, "have the courage for once to show your side. You will be welcome to come over to our side once you are truly ashamed of your own. Not until then. Let us have no hypocrisy."

(2) "Will all those who love the Lord Jesus Christ stand up? Now, please, be careful. Act conscientiously, lest God's judgment fall upon you. Those who truly love the Lord Jesus—and they only."

Again a great crowd responds, and to the query, "Do you really and truly love him?" there comes a loud, triumphant answer, "Yes."

(3) "Now for the question which Christ put to Peter. It is now put to you individually. Do you love Jesus 'more than these'—more than all things?"

It's a crucial moment—the query is so startling and unexpected. There is a momentary hesitation, and then once more the congregation is on its feet, and there is a joyful, triumphant rendering of "Diadem."

> Bring forth the royal diadem
> And crown him Lord of all.

"You have made a great declaration—you love him more than all things, all things. We shall presently see how sincere is the declaration. We shall see it in crowded attendances at prayer-meetings, at church-meetings. We shall see

it in the daily study of God's own Book. We shall no
longer hear the old excuse, ' No time to read the Bible.'
Have you time to eat ? The needs of the body are attended
to, but, bobol anwyl, what of the sustenance of the soul that
is so much more precious ? The soul ever thirsts for God.
You must be in touch with God's Word every day, every
day, were it only one verse."

Have all obeyed the third command to stand up? No,
not all. A few are sitting. The test is too severe. " One
has gone out," exclaims a voice in the gallery ; " he cannot
stand it."

" Bring him back, Lord, bring him back," prays a young
fellow of nineteen near the door. " Do n't let thy judgment
fall upon him. He has felt the Spirit moving—he said so
—but he is fleeing. Bring him back." " He will come
back, friend," the missioner assures us, " he will come back ;
the fact that he has run away is a proof that he will come
back."

The next question is one that gives relief —

(4) " All those who want to love the Lord Jesus, will
they stand up ? "

There is now not a single seat occupied. Members,
non-members, sceptics, scoffers—all, all are on their feet,
and the silence that supervenes is oppressive. But the missioner is all happiness and smiles.

Presently we are singing that inspiring hymn of praise —

> Duw mawr y rhyfeddodau maith
> Rhyfeddol yw pob rhan o'th waith,

and we are reminded by the missioner that in that hymn we
are addressing God himself, and that if we cannot sing with
all our hearts we had better be silent.

In the same issue the reporter publishes a special message
given him by Mr. Roberts for the public. After emphatically disclaiming any share in the religious upheaval, which
he attributed solely to the Holy Spirit, Mr. Roberts said :

" I will give you a message. I should like the people to
believe. They wait for me. They should wait only for

the Spirit. Some one said they are almost breaking their
hearts for me to go. Will they almost break their hearts for
the Holy Spirit? Then it must come down. What does
the Word say? 'Ask and receive.' It is just that. 'Ask
and ye shall receive.' That is the promise. Believe it.
Don't wait for me. Some are talking of the share that this
denomination or that has in the work. It is not denomina-
tional. In Loughor we had all denominations—Methodists,
Churchmen, Congregationalists, Baptists, every one."

" Give me a message distinct, plain, for the people, Mr.
Roberts."

He waited a minute or two before answering, and then
said :

" This is the message. Of course I had to pray for it.
To ask for guidance how the prophecy of Joel is being fulfilled. There the Lord says, ' I will pour out my Spirit
upon all flesh.' If that be so all flesh must be prepared to
receive it. Note the four conditions :

" First. The past must be clear : every sin confessed
to God. Any wrong put upon any man must be made
right.

" Second. Everything doubtful must be removed once
and for all out of our lives.

" Third. Obedience prompt and implicit to the Holy
Spirit.

" Fourth. Public confession must be made of Christ.

" These are the four conditions given. If every church,
will comply with these four conditions, then all will be made
one. Once the Spirit comes down and takes possession of
a man, he is made one with Christ and one with all men.
All denominations are one. You know what Christ said,
' I, if I be lifted up, will draw all men unto me.' There it
is. Christ is all in all."

Mr. Roberts indulges in no invectives against anything

or anybody. He does not even denounce the publican. At one meeting, on December 4th, he heard a young fellow declaring, "A week ago I was blind drunk; to-day I am free, and the craving is gone." "Aye, aye," exclaims the missioner, "and there's no need to preach against the drink; but preach Christ, proclaim Christ unto the people: that is all-sufficient."

The truth about Evan Roberts is that he is very psychic, with clairvoyance well developed and a strong visualizing gift. One peculiarity about him is that he has not yet found any watch that will keep time when it is carried in his pocket. Many of his visions are merely the vivid visualization of mental concepts, as, for instance, when he says:

"When I go out to the garden I see the devil grinning at me, but I am not afraid of him; I go into the house, and when I go out again to the back I see Jesus Christ smiling at me. Then I know all is well."

This, again, is much the same thing:

While listening to a sermon at Newcastle Emlyn once, he said, he received much more of the Spirit of the gospel from what he saw than from what he heard. The preacher was doing very well, was warming with his work, and sweating by the very energy of his delivery. And when he (Evan Roberts) saw the sweat on the preacher's brow he looked beyond and saw another vision: his Lord sweating the bloody sweat in the garden (and then, as Mr. Roberts thought of the "vision," he utterly broke down).

The missioners go like the Friars of old, or like the Seventy in the gospel, without money and without scrip. As Sir A. Thomas said, the revival finances itself. There are no bills, no halls, no salaries.

CHAPTER V

THE RISE AND PROGRESS OF THE REVIVAL

MR. GEORGE MEREDITH once remarked that one great secret of the triumph of Christianity over the paganism of imperial Rome was the astonishing discovery made by the Apostle Paul as to the value of women as religious teachers. Before his time women served in the sanctuary indeed, but as creatures of sense, for the degradation rather than as embodiments of souls capable of inspiring and uplifting the human race. Paul, it is true, when introducing so great an innovation, found it necessary, while addressing the Church of Corinth, to draw a very hard and fast line limiting the sphere of female activity; and this limitation, which was local and temporary, being necessitated solely by the corruption of sex morality in Corinth at that time, has been used, no doubt to the apostle's infinite chagrin, to limit the beneficent action of women in the ministry of the Church in other ages and in other climes. Christianity, however, is at last sloughing the Corinthian limitation and asserting the full freedom which Paul secured for women elsewhere. The Quakers began the good work. The Methodists did something in the same direction. It was reserved for the Salvation Army, the only religious organization founded by a husband and wife acting in absolute unity, to make the equality of the sexes a chief corner-stone. Now in South Wales we see the fruits of this devoted testimony. The Welsh, down to the time of the last revival, were in the bonds of the Corinthian limitation. Even in the sixties a lady lecturer on temperance was looked at askance in many parts of Wales.

Now all that has gone by the board. In the present revival women are everywhere to the fore, singing, testifying, praying and preaching. Dr. Henry Rees, who protested publicly in 1866 against the ministry of women, appears to be dead, and his spirit has died with him. At last these good people have realized the great saying that as in Christ there is neither bond nor free, so there is neither male nor female. The change is so marked that it suggests the happy thought that as the revival of 1859 to 1861 led to the enfranchisement of the male householder, the present revival may be crowned by the recognition by the State of the full citizenship of women.

Women came into this revival chiefly as singers, but they soon found that the ministry of sacred song needed to be supplemented by that of prayer and of exhortation. But even if they had done nothing but sing, they would have had a leading part in this revival. For it is as Dr. Joseph Parry predicted, as long ago as 1891, that it would be a singing revival.

How did it begin, this revival? Where was it nursed into being? What influences nurtured it into the full maturity of its powers?

For a long time past the Welsh Christians had been moved to pray specially for the quickening of religious life in their midst. The impulse appears to have been sporadic and spontaneous. In remote country hamlets, in mining villages buried in distant valleys, one man or one woman would have it laid upon his or her soul to pray that the Holy Spirit might be poured out upon the cause in which they were spiritually concerned. There does not seem to have been much organized effort. It was all individual, local, and strictly limited to the neighborhood.

But prayer circles formed by devout persons who agree to unite together in prayer at a given hour every day have long been a recognized form of prevailing prayer. By these circles there are some thirty or forty thousand people now banded together to pray for a world-wide revival.

All this was general. It was preparing the way. A great longing for revival was abroad in the land. The churches were conscious that there was something in the air. It was at New Quay, in Cardiganshire, that the spark appears to have first fired the charged train of religious emotion. Fortunately, we have from the Rev. Joseph Jenkins, the pastor of the Calvinistic church in which the revival first made its appearance, an authentic account of its beginning. The first person to be awakened was the pastor himself. He was a good man, a devoted Christian, and a faithful minister; but, like Evan Roberts, he felt that there was still something lacking. It was before midsummer, 1903, that the conviction was borne in upon the good pastor's mind that the occasion had come for special services with greater freedom for testifying. It was his own quickened spiritual experience which sought the institution of these meetings as a means of giving expression to the life of the church.

The meetings he had in view were to have no set form. They must be free, each to assume its own peculiar form spontaneously. Those present would be expected to pray, sing, read or speak, according to the impulse of the moment. He longed to pour his spiritual experience into sympathetic ears. He found himself frequently in close communion with his heavenly Father, and seemed to be given everything necessary to efficient service. He related his experience in fear and trembling. He felt that he himself must have been saved many years ago, although he had missed the joy which the knowledge of such a fact brings. He had no doubt that his efforts to preach Christ had been honest, and that he had done his best to obtain for himself also some of the benefits of his preaching. And yet he had never before understood the gospel as he understands it to-day—the power of God unto present assurance of full salvation.

Some time ago—the preacher was speaking in November, and his sermon was reported in *The South Wales Daily News* of November 16th, and no more precise date is given—the experience occurred which may be regarded as the first outward and visible sign of the revival. I give the story as it is reported. A "Seiat" appears to be a religious meeting for prayer:

Some time ago he had returned from a journey, and found that a "Seiat" had been set aside in favor of a soirée to be held in the town. Somebody rose at one of the church meetings and asked why the "Seiat" was being set aside—the soirée was not a sufficient reason. It was decided to hold a "Seiat," and in that meeting were seen and heard the first indications of the dayspring from on high that was surely dawning upon the church. A young girl prayed, and that prayer was the most wonderful and touching he had ever heard. The response was immediate. All were lifted up into a high plane of spiritual experience. One of the older deacons, who was standing by the door, came forward. Hot tears were rolling down his face when he said, "It's all right, I know him. He is the Holy Spirit."

The minister as he sat marveled at the signs of the new experience that he knew must be coming to the church. Nevertheless, his heart was not perfectly right before the Lord. A brother minister with whom he had spent a night had, in course of conversation upon religious matters, said to him very straightforwardly, "My friend, I am afraid you are backsliding; there is something in your view of things, and in the cadences of your voice, that betokens serious backsliding in your spiritual life." It was too true, he ad-

mitted—and the charge went home. The conviction of its
truth and of its guilt sank deep into his soul. A bosom
friend—Mr. Ceredig Evans—to whom he told his experience, wept and prayed with him, and promised to continue at the throne of grace on his behalf. He was perfectly convinced that the matter of his soul as between
himself and God was not settled altogether in God's way.
A Voice within him demanded work of him, demanded the
fulfilment of his ministry. He was shown others with
humbler talents, as he was told, yet with far better records
of real work done in the Master's vineyard. His wife was
present, and knew all his private experience in this matter—
how he prayed all night, and night after night continued
to pray and read, until one night in his study, in the small
hours of the morning, a vision of the cross arose filling his
soul with joy and peace.

Here again we have the vision. "In point of fact," says
Professor James, "you will hardly find a religious leader of
any kind in whose life there is no record of such things.
St. Paul had his visions, his ecstasies, his gift of tongues.
The whole array of Christian saints and heresiarchs, including the greatest, the Bernards, the Loyolas, the Luthers,
the Foxes, the Wesleys, had these visions, voices, rapt conditions, guiding impressions, and openings. They had these
things because they had exalted sensibility, and to such
things persons of exalted sensibility are liable."

Pastor Jenkins, having thus entered into a new and fuller relation with the Spirit, summoned his young people to the
new kind of meetings which he saw were called for. They
were well attended, and were conducted on the principle of
leaving every one free to pray, sing, and speak, or sit silent
as the Spirit moved him.

One Sunday night he preached from the text, "This is
the victory that overcometh the world, even our faith."

He had preached before on some phases of that subject, but now he felt his very soul go out in his words, which God blessed immediately. That night a young girl came to his house to consult him concerning the salvation of her soul. She did not know how she should speak to him, and remained walking to and fro outside the house for some time. But she was intensely in earnest, and, courage coming, she entered the house. He advised her to receive Jesus as her Saviour, but that she must receive him as Lord as well as Saviour—she must surrender all to him. She must pray until her soul allowed the matter to be settled on God's terms. She promised to follow his advice, and she did, for her soul was moved to its lowest depth. A Christian Endeavor meeting was coming, and he would then see how far they understood spiritual experience. He spoke, explaining it in the best way he could, and with all the force at his command. Others followed with speeches, but he required of them expressions of spiritual experience pure and simple, and then it was that the young girl already referred to stood up, and with beaming face and thrilling voice said, "Oh, I love Jesus with all my heart." After this, spiritual history was made rapidly at the Christian Endeavor meetings, some revealing great depths of emotion, others manifesting the keenest sense of spiritual relations.

That public confession of her faith by the young girl—who may be regarded as the first convert of the revival—was followed by others. It was evident the revival had come. One Christian Endeavorer, who had prepared a paper to read on the existence of God, could not bring himself to read it for the same reason that Professor James dismisses the arguments of philosophy as a foundation for religion. He said that spiritually the meeting was far in advance of his paper. The Christian Endeavorers had the proofs of his existence in their own hearts. There was no shadow of doubt of his existence. He was there amongst them then, transforming their very lives. In this way their meetings were started. From New Quay, which lies midway been Cardigan and Aberystwyth, the Christian Endeavorers went out to hold meetings elsewhere. Among other places, they went to Newcastle Emlyn, where they met Evan Roberts.

So far as I can fix it from the materials at my disposal, the public confession of the young girl which marks the beginning of the revival occurred in New Quay in February, 1904.

It was in September that Evan Roberts prayed at the New Quay Christian Endeavorers' meeting and saw the visions which directed him to Loughor. It was in the beginning of November he began to hold the special services. at Loughor, which attracted the attention of the press. After that the full reports of the proceedings in *The Western Mail* and *The Cardiff Daily News* spread the revival through the whole of South Wales.

It is worthy of note that the great revival of 1859 also began in Cardiganshire, although somewhat farther to the north than New Quay. The following notes as to the places visited by Mr. Evan Roberts will give those who know the district, but to no one else, some idea how the fire spread along the valleys of Wales.

November 14th and 15th, Trecynon ; November 16th to 18th, Pontycymmer ; November 19th, Bridgend, Pyle, Abergwynfi ; November 20th, Abercynon ; November 21st and 22d, Mountain Ash ; November 23d and 24th, Ynysybwl ; November 25th, ill ; November 26th, Cilfyngdd ; November 27th and 28th, Porth ; November 29th, Treorky ; December 2d to 4th, Pentre ; December 5th and 6th, Caerphilly ; December 7th, Senghenydd ; December 8th to 10th, Ferndale ; December 11th, Mardy ; December 12th and 13th,

Tylorstown; December 14th and 15th, Aberfan; December 16th and 17th, Hafod (Pontypridd); December 18th, Pontypridd; December 19th and 20th, Clydach Vale; December 21st, Tonypandy; December 22d, Penygraig; December 23d, Treherbert.

"The supreme test of a revival," says the Rev. F. B. Meyer, "is the ethical result." As to this, the testimony of all on the spot is unanimous. Not merely are all the grosser vices reduced to vanishing point, but the subtler sins of unforgiving rancor, non-payment of debts, dishonest work are abated. In nothing is Mr. Evan Roberts clearer and more emphatic than in his insistence upon forgiveness of injuries, unless it be as to the duty of the payment of debts. "It's no use asking God to forgive you," he tells his hearers, "unless you have forgiven all your enemies— every one. You will only be forgiven in the same measure as you forgive." Again he says: "How can there be, when there are family feuds and personal animosities, churches torn by little dissensions, members cold towards each other? If you are not prepared to forgive others it is no use going on your knees to-night to ask God to forgive your transgressions. I don't say don't do it; please yourselves, of course; but one thing is absolutely certain, God will not listen to you."

The result has been excellent—everywhere excellent.

However we may explain it, the veriest sceptic must admit that what the revivalist seeks to effect is of all things the most important object of human endeavor. No political or social change can be regarded as having any serious importance, excepting so far as it tends to facilitate indirectly the achievement of the same result which the revivalist seeks directly. The aim of all reformers is the regeneration of the individual. To make a bad man good, a cruel man merciful, a lazy man industrious, a drunkard sober, and to substitute selfless struggle to help others for a selfish scramble to seize everything for oneself—that in the aim-all, the be-all, and the end-all of all those who seek the improvement of society and the progress of the world. It makes no difference whether the reformer is called Blatchford or Liddon, Bradlaugh or Price Hughes, John Morley or General Booth, Frederic Harrison or the Archbishop of Canterbury, the President of the Free Thinkers' Congress or the Pope of Rome—that is what they are all after—that, and in the ultimate, nothing but that. And when it comes to be looked at scientifically, who can deny that a great religious revival often succeeds in achieving the result which we all desire more rapidly, more decisively, and in a greater number of cases, than any other agency known to mankind? We may discount it as much as we like, but the facts are there. It is not necessary to credit the revival with all the results which it reveals, any more than we may credit a day's sunshine in spring with all the flowers it brings to birth. But it brings them out. So does a revival. And if there had been no revival, the latent sainthood of multitudes would never have been born, just as the flowers would never come out in May if there were no sun.

It is often argued that revivalism is ephemeral. But as our brief historical retrospect shows, the fruits of revivals are among the most permanent things in history.

CHAPTER VI

WHAT OUGHT I TO DO?

SPREAD the good news, and spread it now!

If you can do nothing else, send copies of this pamphlet to any relative, friend or other person whom you think may become interested in the subject. Speak to people about it. Write to your friends about it.

If you belong to a church, try to get the members interested in the revival.

If you are a minister, preach about it, and ask your people to hold prayer-meetings on the subject.

For if those who have seen most of the revival are right, there is a great blessing in this movement for each of us, and for all of us, if we but make the most of our present opportunity.

What we have to do is to take time by the forelock and be ready to clutch the boon before the moment has passed. As a start, we might well begin each in our sphere by doing good turns to our enemies, wiping out the memories of old grudges, reconciling offended relatives, and forgiving others, even as we hope to be forgiven.

God or no God, soul or no soul, this earth is made much more like hell than heaven by persisting in these grudges, jealousies, animosities, and unkind feelings one toward another. What a merry Christmas, what a glad New Year it would be if we could begin by being in charity with everybody, in love with every man, woman and child with whom we have a personal acquaintance!

Then when we have cast out from our own souls the evil

73

spirits of bitterness, rancor, unfriendliness, jealousy, and have forgiven all those who have injured us, or, a much harder task, whom we have injured, we shall be better prepared to receive the outpouring of the divine blessing which we all profess to desire.

After the revival has come, as come it will if we but make room for it by ejecting hatred, malice and uncharitableness from our hearts, then a great duty will be laid upon the churches to supply fresh interests for the new converts, who have given up everything that filled their leisure. The Rev. Dr. Morris, of Treorky, and ex-president of the Baptist Union, told an interviewer of *The South Wales Daily News* that he at least is fully alive to the importance of this subject:

"Do you know," he said, "this revival has thrown a tremendous responsibility upon the churches? Public-houses and football fields are being emptied of young men. What are the churches going to do with them? Unfortunately, we in Wales are lamentably deficient in provision for the development of the body, mind and spirit of a man. I agree absolutely with the leading articles in *The South Wales Daily News*, when they urge that Christianity should provide for the education and development of the whole of a man, and not merely a part of him. The churches have been brought face to face with a difficult problem. How shall we keep our young people, now that they have been induced to join the church? In small places there is no attraction in the church; no accommodation is attempted for their moral well-being."

"What would you suggest as a means of meeting this contingency?"

"My suggestion would be the provision of an institutional church. There should be young men's and young women's parlors, separate classrooms, lecture-rooms, museums, and libraries. I would also advise the encouragement of physical culture—of course, we must guard against extremes—but some means must be devised to hold our young

people, otherwise a great part of the good effect of the revival will be lost."

Upon this question possibly some hints may be gained
from my Christmas story, "Here Am I: Send Me!"

II

The Revival: Its Power and Source

The Revival: Its Power and Source

By Rev. G. Campbell Morgan, D. D., London

[We are permitted by Dr. Morgan, who controls the copyright, to condense into the following article a recent sermon by him to his people at Westminster Chapel, London, and published in the *Christian Commonwealth.*—EDITORS.]

IT was my holy privilege to come into the center of this wonderful work and movement. Arriving in the morning in the village, everything seemed quiet, and we wended our way to the place where a group of chapels stood. Oh, these chapels through Wales! Thank God for them! Everything was so quiet and orderly that we had to ask where the meeting was. A lad, pointing to a chapel, said, "In there." Not a single person outside. We made our way through the open door, and just managed to get inside, and found the chapel crowded from floor to ceiling with a great mass of people.

THE THREE CHARACTERISTICS OF THE MEETINGS

It was a meeting characterized by a perpetual series of interruptions and disorderliness. It was a meeting characterized by a great continuity and an absolute order. You say, "How do you reconcile these things?" I do not reconcile them. They are both there. If you put a man into the midst of one of these meetings who knows nothing of the language of the Spirit, and nothing of the life of the Spirit, one of two things will happen to him. He will either pass out saying, "These men are drunk," or he himself will be swept up by the fire into the kingdom of God. If you put a man down who knows the language of the Spirit, he will be struck by this most peculiar thing. I have never seen anything like it in my life; while a man praying is disturbed by the breaking out of song, there is no sense of disorder, and the prayer merges into song, and back into testimony, and back again into song for hour after hour, without guidance. These are the three occupations—singing, prayer, testimony.

In the afternoon we were at another chapel, and another meeting, equally full, and this time Evan Roberts was present. He came into the meeting when it had been on for an hour and a half. He spoke, but his address—if it could be called an address—was punctuated perpetually by song and prayer and testimony. Evan Roberts works on that plan, never hindering any one. I venture to say that if that address Evan Roberts gave in broken fragments had been reported, the whole of it could have been read in six or seven minutes. As the meeting went on, a man rose in the gallery and said, "So and So," naming some man, "has decided for Christ," and then in a moment the song began. They did not sing Songs of Praises, they sang Diolch Iddo, and the weirdness and beauty of it swept over the audience. It was a song of praise because that man was born again. There are no inquiry rooms, no penitent forms, but some worker announces, or an inquirer openly confesses Christ, the name is registered and the song breaks out, and they go back to testimony and prayer.

In the evening I stood for three solid hours wedged so that I could not lift my hands at all. That which impressed me most was the congregation. I stood wedged, and I looked along the gallery of the chapel on my right, and there were three women, and the rest were men packed solidly in. If you could but for once have seen the men, evidently colliers, with the blue seam that told of their work on their faces, clean and beautiful. Beautiful, did I say? Many of them lit with heaven's own light, radiant with the light that never was on sea and land. Great rough, magnificent, poetic men by nature, but the nature had slumbered long. To-day it is awakened, and I looked on many a face, and I knew that men did not see me, did not see Evan Roberts, but they saw the face of God and the eternities. I left that evening, after having been in the meeting three hours, at 10:30, and it swept on, packed as it was, until an early hour next morning, song and prayer and testimony and conversion and confession of sin by leading church-members publicly, and the putting of it away, and all the while no human leader, no one indicating the next thing to do, no one checking the spontaneous movement.

The Man Himself

Evan Roberts is hardly more than a boy, simple and natural, no orator; with nothing of the masterfulness that characterized such men as Wesley and Whitefield and Dwight Lyman Moody; no leader of men. One of the most brilliant writers in one of our papers said of Evan Roberts, in a tone of sorrow, that he lacked the qualities of leadership, and the writer said if but some prophet did now arise he could sweep everything before him. God has not chosen that a prophet shall arise. It is quite true. Evan Roberts is no orator, no leader. What is he? I mean now with regard to this great movement. He is the mouthpiece of the fact that there is no human guidance as to man or organization. The burden of what he says to the people is this: It is not man; do not wait for me; depend on God; obey the Spirit. But whenever moved to do so, he speaks under the guidance of the Spirit. His work is not that of appealing to men so much as that of creating an atmosphere by calling men to follow the guidance of the Spirit in whatever the Spirit shall say to them.

God has set his hand upon the lad, beautiful in simplicity, ordained in his devotion, lacking all the qualities that we have looked for in preachers and prophets and leaders. He has put him in the forefront of this movement that the world may see that he does choose the things that are not to bring to naught the things that are, the weak things of the world to confound the things that are mighty; a man who lacks all the essential qualities which we say make for greatness, in order that through him in simplicity and power he may move to victory.

Peculiarities of the Movement

There is no preaching, no order, no hymn books, no choirs, no organs, no collections and, finally, no advertising. I am not saying these things are wrong. I simply want you to see what God is doing. There were the organs, but silent; the ministers, but among the rest of the people, rejoicing and prophesying with the rest, only there was no preaching. Everybody is preaching. No order, and yet it moves from day to day, week to week, county to county, with matchless precision, with the order of an attacking force. Mr. Stead was asked if he thought the revival would spread to London, and he said, "It depends upon whether you can sing." He was not so wide of the mark. When these Welshmen sing, they sing the words like men who believe them. They abandon themselves to their singing. We sing as though we thought it would not be respectable to be heard by the man next to us. No choir, did I say? It was all choir. And hymns! I stood and listened in wonder and amazement as that congregation on that night sang hymn after hymn, long hymns, sung through without hymn-books.

The Sunday-school is having its harvest now. The family altar is having its harvest now. The teaching of hymns and the Bible among those Welsh hills and valleys is having its harvest now. No advertising. The whole thing advertises itself. You tell me the press is advertising it. They did not begin advertising until the thing caught fire and spread. One of the most remarkable things is the attitude of the Welsh press. I come across instance after instance of men converted by reading the story of the revival in *The Western Mail* and *The South Wales Daily News*.

THE ORIGIN OF THE MOVEMENT

In the name of God let us all cease trying to find it. At least let us cease trying to trace it to any one man or convention. You cannot trace it, and yet I will trace it to-night. Whence has it come? All over Wales—I am giving you roughly the result of the questioning of fifty or more persons at random in the week—a praying remnant have been agonizing before God about the state of the beloved land, and it is through that the answer of fire has come. You tell me that the revival originates with Roberts. I tell you that Roberts is a product of the revival. You tell me that it began in an Endeavor meeting where a dear girl bore testimony. I tell you that was part of the result of a revival breaking out everywhere. If you and I could stand above Wales, looking at it, you would see fire breaking out here and there, and yonder, and somewhere else, without any collusion or prearrangement. It is a divine visitation in which God—let me say this reverently—in which God is saying to us: See what I can do without the things you are depending on; see what I can do in answer to a praying people; see what I can do through the simplest who are ready to fall in line and depend wholly and absolutely upon me.

A Church Revival

What is the character of this revival? It is a church revival. I do not mean by that merely a revival among church members. It is that, but it is held in church buildings. I have been saying for a long time that the revival which is to be permanent in the life of a nation must be associated with the life of the churches. What I am looking for is that there shall come a revival breaking out in all our regular church life. The meetings are held in the chapels, all up and down the valleys, and it began among church-members, and when it touches the outside man it makes him into a church-member at once. I am tremendously suspicious of any mission or revival movement that treats with contempt the Church of Christ, and affects to despise the churches. Within five weeks twenty thousand have joined the churches. I think more than that have been converted, but the churches in Wales have enrolled during the last five weeks twenty thousand new members. It is a movement in the Church and of the Church, a movement in which the true functions and forces of the Church are being exercised and filled.

Striking Cases of Personal Influence

What effect is this work producing upon men? First of all, it is turning Christians everywhere into evangelists. There is nothing more remarkable about it than that, I think. People you never expected to see doing this kind of thing are becoming definite personal workers. A friend of mine went to one of the meetings, and he walked down to the meeting with an old friend of his, a deacon of the Congregational church, a man whose piety no one doubted, a man who for long years had worked in the life of the church in some of its departments, but a man who never would think of speaking to men about their souls, although he would not have objected to some one else doing it. As my friend walked down with the deacon, the deacon said to him : "I have eighteen young men in an athletic class of which I am president. I hope some of them will be in the meeting to-night." There was a new manifestation. This man had had that athletic class for years, and he had never hoped that any one of them would be in any meeting to be saved. Within fifteen minutes he left his seat by my friend and was seen talking to a young man down in front of him. Presently this deacon rose and said, "Thank God for So and So," giving his name; "he has given his heart to Christ right here." In a moment or two he left him, and was with another young man. Before that meeting closed that deacon had led every one of those eighteen young men to Jesus Christ, who never before thought of speaking to men about their souls.

My own friend, with whom I stayed, who has always been reticent of speaking to men, told me how, sitting in his office, there surged upon him the great conviction that he ought to go and speak to another man with whom he had done business for long years. My friend suddenly put down his pen and left his office and went on 'Change, and there he saw the very man ; and going up to him, passing the time of day to him, the man said to him, "What do you think of this revival?" And my friend looked him squarely in the eye and said, "How is it with your own soul?" The man looked back at him and said, "Last night at twelve, for some unknown reason, I had to get out of bed and give myself to Jesus Christ, and I was hungering for some one to come and talk to me." Here is a man turned into an evangelist by supernatural means. If this is emotional, then God send us more of it ! Here is a cool, calculating, business ship owner, that I have known all my life, leaving his office to go on 'Change and ask a man about his soul.

Down in one of the mines a collier was walking along, and he came, to his great surprise, to where one of the principal officials in the mine was standing. The official said, "Jim, I have been waiting two hours here for you." "Have you, sir?" said Jim. "What do you want?" "I want to be saved, Jim." The man said, "Let us get right down here"; and there in the mine the colliery official, instructed by the collier, passed into the kingdom of God. When he got up he said, "Tell all the men, tell everybody you meet, I am converted."

The movement is characterized by the most remarkable confession of sin—confessions that must be costly. I heard some of them, men rising who have been members of the church and officers of the church, confessing hidden sin in their heart, impurity committed and condoned, and seeking prayer for its putting away. The whole movement is marvelously characterized by a confession of Jesus Christ, testimony to his power, to his goodness, to his beneficence, and testimony merging forevermore into outbursts of singing.

This whole thing is of God; it is a visitation in which he is making men conscious of Himself, without any human agency. The revival is far more wide-spread than the fire zone. In this sense you may understand that the fire zone is where the meetings are actually held, and where you feel the flame that burns. But even when you come out of it, and go into railway trains, or into a shop, a bank, anywhere, men everywhere are talking of God. Whether they obey or not is another matter. There are thousands not yielded to the constraint of God, but God has given Wales in these days a new conviction and consciousness of himself. That is the profound thing, the underlying truth.

CPSIA information can be obtained
at www.ICGtesting.com
Printed in the USA
LVHW091340141118
597108LV00001B/86/P